Country Houses of Lancashire

and their builders

by
John Champness

Centre for North-West Regional Studies
Lancaster University
2011
Series Editor: Sam Riches

Country Houses of Lancashire and their builders

This volume is the 58th in a series of Occasional Papers published by the Centre for North-West Regional Studies at the University of Lancaster

Text Copyright © John Champness 2011

Designed, typeset, printed and bound by
4Word Ltd, Bristol

British Library Cataloguing in-Publication Data
A CIP catalogue entry for this book is available from the British Library

ISBN 978-1-86220-292-4

The majority of images in this book are derived from the author's personal collection. Additional images were taken by Gwen Ainsworth of Folio, Lancaster University's Photographic Unit. These are: 0.1, 3.18, 3.19, 3.20, 6.0, 6.11, 6.12, 6.16, 6.29, 6.30, 7.2, 7.5. The ground plans were prepared by Andrew Malby.

The author and publisher gratefully acknowledge Dr Philip Welch's financial support for the illustrations of this book.

Dedication

This book is dedicated, with affectionate thanks, to two long-standing friends: to Suzie Reynolds, the *châtelaine* of Leighton Hall, who suggested my name as a tutor on country houses to the Lancaster University Summer Programme in 1985; and to Oliver Westall, then the Director of the University's Centre for North-West Regional Studies, who has almost ever since been encouraging me to write on the subject as well.

John Champness

John Champness 1939–2011: an appreciation

John Champness, the author and 'onelie begetter' of this book, was born in 1939 at Staveley in Derbyshire, where his father was a stationmaster. The family soon afterwards soon moved to London, where John was educated at the City of London School. He went on to Jesus College, Cambridge, where he read French and German, and then taught for a short time in London before moving to Warwick School in 1964. In 1967 (the year he married Doreen) he became senior French master at Sedbergh but in 1970 left teaching and began a new career as an architectural and buildings historian. This had always been one of his passions: now it became his life's work.

He was appointed first as North West Regional Secretary for the Royal Institute of British Architects, based in Manchester. From there he went on to the Civic Trust for the North West and then in 1974 to the planning department of Lancashire County Council, where he eventually became the County Conservation Officer. John lectured for many years on the Lancaster University Summer Programme, and organised day and weekend courses on country houses and church architecture for Barlaston College in Staffordshire and other colleges, as well as independently. In 1998 he retired from the County Council after almost 25 years of guiding and overseeing its policies towards Lancashire's built heritage. In his contented retirement John continued to research, write, lecture and teach. He wrote a number of important works on aspects of the architectural history and heritage of Lancashire, several of them published by the County Council in those halcyon days when local authorities were allowed to be enlightened and to spend modest sums on worthy projects.

1977	*A walk round historic Lancaster* (privately published; and later editions)
1983	*Lancashire's early industrial heritage* (Lancashire County Planning Department; and later editions)
1984	*Churches in the Lancaster area* (Lancaster City Council)

1984   *Historic houses in the Lancaster area* (Lancaster City Council)

1989   *Lancashire* (Shire County Guides)

1989   *Lancashire's architectural heritage: an anthology of fine buildings* (Lancashire County Planning Department)

1993   *Lancaster Castle: a brief history* (Lancaster County Books)

2005   *Thomas Harrison: Georgian architect of Chester and Lancaster 1744–1829* (Centre for North West Regional Studies, Lancaster University)

For many years John had been planning this present book, intending that it would bring together much of his archival research in documents and illustrations, linking that with an unrivalled personal knowledge of the buildings 'on the ground' which resulted from visiting, exploring, mapping and drawing the country houses of the historic county. The book gradually took shape, and I was privileged to be asked to work with John as editor of the volume, acting as an adviser, reader, occasional critic and frequent sounding-board as he tried out different approaches and honed and polished his text. I had known John for many years before then, and it was a real pleasure to share this with him. In conversations, notes and drafts of text he opened my eyes and as he explained his thinking (and as, at his home, I drank the best coffee in Lancaster) I found my own understanding of the subject growing clearer.

John's philosophy about architecture was simple, but is surprisingly rare. He considered that far too much written on the subject is pretentious, over-complicated and burdened with obscure jargon and technical terms. His view was that, as a result, the general reader is often deterred from finding out more (he mentioned, for example, how guidebooks to monastic sites still sometimes use the coy and decorous term 'reredorter' to describe what is much more satisfactorily labelled 'communal latrine block').

Even more importantly, though, John also believed passionately that in order to make buildings explicable, it is necessary to consider how they actually worked and to ask questions. He would interrogate a country house: why is it laid out in that particular way; what function did the particular elements perform and how did they interact; was this or that feature purely decorative, or were there other reasons for its existence; what technical or structural reasons were there for the shape, height, layout and appearance; how did the use of certain materials affect the building process ... these and many other questions, interpreted by John, made a house much more than just a three-dimensional structure. It acquired a personality, a biography.

And there was more, for John also recognised that houses are nothing, and would not exist, without the people who built them and occupied them. So more questions might and should be asked – about the family origins, status, income, aspirations, household size, upward or downward mobility, and cultural and dynastic contacts of families and individuals. Since so many Lancashire houses met, in the twentieth century, with fates of varying sadness, from conversion to dereliction to demolition, he would ask more whys and wherefores. But he was neither sentimental nor unrealistic about this – he once said to me that the loss of so many timber-framed manor houses in the south of the county in the period from 1920 to 1980 was probably both historically inevitable and even in some (only 'some') ways not a bad thing. If we had had 200 such houses, he said, we wouldn't value them, but as we have fewer than 20 the survivors should be treasured.

John was a gifted communicator, blessed with the instinctive ability to translate the complicated into clear and simple description and explanation. He was endlessly curious, enquiring about the details of buildings, identifying new sources, locating hitherto unknown drawings. For John, there was never a point at which research and investigation was complete – only a point where, for practical reasons, it had to be temporarily suspended. With many of the houses described in this book there were further explorations to be made, and questions to be answered, but he realised that at some point the text had to be put down on paper. He was the kindest and most courteous of men, willing to be criticised (though fighting his case vigorously) and always anxious to help with information. He campaigned strongly for heritage, ecology and green issues, and his contribution to Lancashire's history and heritage was important in his lifetime and will last long into the future.

To have worked with John was a privilege, as many know to their benefit. For me, it was richly rewarding. He was such a good man, as well as hugely knowledgeable. As was said almost 300 years ago of one of the greatest of all English architects, and can equally well be said of this book, *Lector, si monumentum requiris, circumspice.*[1]

Alan Crosby

---

[1]   'Reader, if you seek his memorial, look around you.' This tribute is written on the monument to Sir Christopher Wren (died 1723) in St Paul's Cathedral, London.

Contents

Acknowledgements

This book could not have been contemplated, let alone completed, without the generous help and encouragement of a large number of people. It is therefore a pleasure to thank:

Firstly, 'generations' of adult students at the Lancaster University Summer Programme, at Alston Hall Residential College and at the Wedgwood Memorial College at Barlaston;

Secondly, the Editorial Board of the Centre for North-West Regional Studies who accepted my draft for publication;

Thirdly, as individuals (in alphabetical order), the many house owners or curators who have answered my questions and checked the relevant parts of my text, and dozens of friends who share my interest and have discussed the subject and my interpretations with me over many years or have otherwise helped me: Gwen Ainsworth, Hal and Susan Bagot, Anthony Blacklay, Susan Bourne, David Brazendale, David Brock, Grania Cavendish, Lesley Chappells, Simon Chew, Roman Cizdyn, Alison Copeland, John Cowap, Alan Crosby, Janet Currie, John Darlington, Richard Dean, Peter de Figueiredo, Mike Derbyshire, Lisa Downes, Roger Dyson, Jeanette Edgar, Liz Fawcett, Emmeline Garnett, John Goodall, Ivan Hall, Clare Hartwell, Kathy Haslam, Helen Hitchings, Bernard de Hoghton, Neil Holt, George Howson, Peter Iles, Fiona Jenkins, Geraldine Johnston, Paul Jones, Frank Kelsall, Terry Kitto, David Knight, Miles Lambert, Jenny Loveridge, Leona Lyons, Andrew Malby, Rachel Malloch, Sally Manfredi, Louise McCall, Marion McClintock, Gary Miller, John Miller, Nigel Morgan, Michael Oppenheim, Vicki Oyston, Robert Parker, Jan Petersen, Dorothy and Gordon Phillips, Keith Piercy, Anne Pinder, Philip Powell, James Price, Clare Pye, Jonathan Ratter, Terry Redding, Richard and Suzie Reynolds, Sam Riches, Andrea Roberts, Victoria Roberts, John Martin Robinson, Geoffrey Roe, Stephen Sartin, Ruth Shrigley, Charles Singleton, Colin Stansfield, Reg Stoddon, Susan Stuart, Jean Turnbull, Alexandra Wedgwood, Philip Welch, Oliver Westall, Andrew White, Christine Wilkinson, Angus Winchester and Michael Winstanley.

Among the above I owe particular thanks to four old friends – firstly to Nigel Morgan, with whom I discussed gentry houses on and off for twenty years, but who died – all too soon in 2006 – before I could show him my first draft. Of the others two are prominent architectural historians, who have read the whole text and made numerous constructive comments – Clare Hartwell, who has written two of the three revised versions of the 'Pevsners' for Lancashire, and Peter de Figueiredo, who worked for ten years for English Heritage and before that co-authored the standard work on Cheshire's country houses. The third is Alan Crosby, the *doyen* of Lancashire local historians and the representative of the CNWRS Editorial Board, whose perceptive criticisms and wise advice helped to turn my text and photographs into this book. I should, of course, add that any mistakes of fact or interpretation which remain are my fault – for which I apologise – and not theirs.

And then, lastly but by no means least, I wish to express my heartfelt thanks to my wife, Doreen, who has loyally supported and lovingly tolerated me – and my writing – for over forty years.

Lancashire and its Gentry Houses

As the map on the next page shows, 'Lancashire' in this book means not just the traditional County Palatine of Lancaster, which included Liverpool and Manchester and the Furness area, but also that part of the Forest of Bowland which came from the former West Riding of Yorkshire in 1974, plus that large fragment of the old Westmorland which nestles between Cartmel and Kirkby Lonsdale. I have also, in a limited number of cases, referred briefly to some well-known houses in neighbouring counties which are significant to the Lancashire story – mostly houses in the care of the National Trust, which has done so much to protect and interpret many of the best English country houses.

I have shown in the Index the approximate location of each house, which is visible or open to the public, by means of a map-reference. Thus, the first house in the book, Warton Old Rectory, which lies in the National Grid square with the coordinates 49 and 72 on the Ordnance Survey Landranger map number 97, is stated to be at 97/49.72. Like most of the houses in the book, it is also named on the OS map itself.

Not all the houses mentioned are open to the public. Those, which are 'normally' open, are named in **bold type**, when first mentioned in each chapter, but not usually thereafter. However, I have also stated clearly after its name when a visible house is private and therefore not open to visitors. And I have repeated this information in the Index. In these cases, please do not ask for permission to visit. Only owners who have received grant-aid from English Heritage are under an obligation to open their houses; the others live in private houses and are entitled to their privacy. 'An Englishman's house is his castle' is a view which I hold strongly.

The best way to check the opening hours of visitable houses is to consult the current edition of Norman Hudson's *'Historic Houses & Gardens'* guide. Hotels and public houses are, of course, open for the price of a drink.

A Note on the Text

Figures in square brackets – thus [4.7] – refer to illustrations in the text. Superscript numbers – thus [2] – indicate references at the end of each chapter.

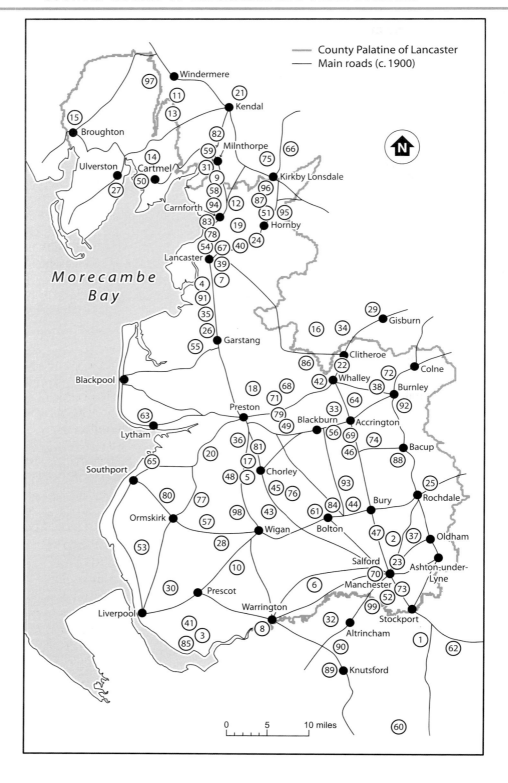

Houses marked on the map

1. Adlington Hall (Cheshire)
2. Alkrington Hall
3. Allerton Hall
4. Ashton Hall
5. Astley Hall (Chorley)
6. Astley Hall (Leigh)
7. Bailrigg House
8. Bank Hall, Warrington (Town Hall)
9. Beetham Hall
10. Birchley Hall
11. Blackwell
12. Borwick Hall
13. Broadleys
14. Broughton Lodge
15. Broughton Tower
16. Browsholme Hall
17. Buckshaw Hall
18. Bushell's Hospital, Goosnargh
19. Capernwray Hall
20. Carr House, Bretherton,
21. Castle Dairy, Kendal
22. Castle Museum (Steward's House), Clitheroe
23. Chetham's Hospital, Manchester
24. Claughton Hall
25. Clegg Hall
26. Clifton Hill
27. Conishead Priory
28. Crawford Manor
29. Cromwell House, Gisburn,
30. Croxteth Hall
31. Dallam Tower
32. Dunham Massey (Cheshire)
33. Dunkenhalgh
34. Eaves Hall
35. Ellel Grange
36. Farington Lodge
37. Foxdenton Hall
38. Gawthorpe Hall
39. Greaves Park, Lancaster
40. Gresgarth Hall
41. Grove House, Allerton
42. Hacking Hall
43. Haigh Hall
44. Hall i' th' Wood
45. Hall o' th' Hill
46. Haworth Art Gallery, Accrington
47. Heaton Hall
48. Heskin Hall
49. Hoghton Tower
50. Holker Hall
51. Hornby Castle
52. Hough End Hall
53. Ince Blundell Hall
54. Judges' Lodgings, Lancaster
55. Kirkland Hall
56. Knuzden Hall
57. Lathom House
58. Leighton Hall
59. Levens Hall
60. Little Moreton Hall (Cheshire)
61. Lostock Hall
62. Lyme Park (Cheshire)
63. Lytham Hall
64. Martholme
65. Meols Hall
66. Middleton Hall
67. Music Room, Lancaster,
68. New Hall, Clayton-le-Dale
69. Oak Hill, Accrington
70. Ordsall Hall
71. Oxendale Hall
72. Park Hill, Barrowford (Pendle Heritage Centre)
73. Platt Hall
74. Rawtenstall Museum
75. Rigmaden Hall
76. Rivington Hall
77. Rufford Old Hall
78. Ryelands House, Lancaster
79. Samlesbury Hall
80. Scarisbrick Hall
81. Shaw Hill Hotel
82. Sizergh Castle
83. Slyne Manor
84. Smithills Hall
85. Speke Hall
86. Stonyhurst
87. Storrs Hall, Arkhome,
88. Stubbylee Hall, Bacup
89. Tabley House (Cheshire)
90. Tatton Park (Cheshire)
91. Thurnham Hall
92. Towneley Hall
93. Turton Tower
94. Warton Old Rectory
95. Wennington Hall
96. Whittington Hall
97. Wray Castle
98. Wrightington Hall
99. Wythenshawe Hall.

0.1. Leighton Hall: a magnificent example of a country house, set in the Lancashire landscape.

Houses marked on the map

1. Adlington Hall (Cheshire)
2. Alkrington Hall
3. Allerton Hall
4. Ashton Hall
5. Astley Hall (Chorley)
6. Astley Hall (Leigh)
7. Bailrigg House
8. Bank Hall, Warrington (Town Hall)
9. Beetham Hall
10. Birchley Hall
11. Blackwell
12. Borwick Hall
13. Broadleys
14. Broughton Lodge
15. Broughton Tower
16. Browsholme Hall
17. Buckshaw Hall
18. Bushell's Hospital, Goosnargh
19. Capernwray Hall
20. Carr House, Bretherton,
21. Castle Dairy, Kendal
22. Castle Museum (Steward's House), Clitheroe
23. Chetham's Hospital, Manchester
24. Claughton Hall
25. Clegg Hall
26. Clifton Hill
27. Conishead Priory
28. Crawford Manor
29. Cromwell House, Gisburn,
30. Croxteth Hall
31. Dallam Tower
32. Dunham Massey (Cheshire)
33. Dunkenhalgh
34. Eaves Hall
35. Ellel Grange
36. Farington Lodge
37. Foxdenton Hall
38. Gawthorpe Hall
39. Greaves Park, Lancaster
40. Gresgarth Hall
41. Grove House, Allerton
42. Hacking Hall
43. Haigh Hall
44. Hall i' th' Wood
45. Hall o' th' Hill
46. Haworth Art Gallery, Accrington
47. Heaton Hall
48. Heskin Hall
49. Hoghton Tower
50. Holker Hall
51. Hornby Castle
52. Hough End Hall
53. Ince Blundell Hall
54. Judges' Lodgings, Lancaster
55. Kirkland Hall
56. Knuzden Hall
57. Lathom House
58. Leighton Hall
59. Levens Hall
60. Little Moreton Hall (Cheshire)
61. Lostock Hall
62. Lyme Park (Cheshire)
63. Lytham Hall
64. Martholme
65. Meols Hall
66. Middleton Hall
67. Music Room, Lancaster,
68. New Hall, Clayton-le-Dale
69. Oak Hill, Accrington
70. Ordsall Hall
71. Oxendale Hall
72. Park Hill, Barrowford (Pendle Heritage Centre)
73. Platt Hall
74. Rawtenstall Museum
75. Rigmaden Hall
76. Rivington Hall
77. Rufford Old Hall
78. Ryelands House, Lancaster
79. Samlesbury Hall
80. Scarisbrick Hall
81. Shaw Hill Hotel
82. Sizergh Castle
83. Slyne Manor
84. Smithills Hall
85. Speke Hall
86. Stonyhurst
87. Storrs Hall, Arkhome,
88. Stubbylee Hall, Bacup
89. Tabley House (Cheshire)
90. Tatton Park (Cheshire)
91. Thurnham Hall
92. Towneley Hall
93. Turton Tower
94. Warton Old Rectory
95. Wennington Hall
96. Whittington Hall
97. Wray Castle
98. Wrightington Hall
99. Wythenshawe Hall.

o.1. Leighton Hall: a magnificent example of a country house, set in the Lancashire landscape.

Introduction

Country houses, as a group, are the finest buildings in Lancashire and a source of great pleasure to many people. My aim in writing this short book is to tell the story of their evolution between the middle of the fourteenth century and the beginning of the twenty-first. Apart from the Earl of Derby's house, Knowsley (which is not open to the public), there are no mansions here like Burghley, Chatsworth or Kedleston. The builders of the finest houses in Lancashire – the men who commissioned the designs and paid for the craftsmen to carry them out – were not peers of the realm, but gentlemen who owned no more than a middle-sized estate and did not aspire to play a rôle outside the county, unless perhaps as an MP. The houses of such men are often called 'gentry houses', and this is the term which I shall use.

This book is not a gazetteer of all gentry houses in Lancashire or even a room-by-room guide to the best of them. I have, instead, looked at the subject more generally, with the aim of explaining how the designs and decorations of these houses (as a group) were developed over those six centuries, and how they reflected the lives, the attitudes and the aspirations of their builders. I have done this by describing, briefly and in a roughly chronological order, important features in a hundred or so of the most attractive and interesting houses which can be visited regularly or can be seen from a public road or footpath. These houses form a good representative sample of surviving gentry houses in Lancashire – and, indeed, in England as a whole. Lancashire is the source of my examples, but the story is in fact similar in most other English counties.

Visiting gentry houses is enjoyable, and studying them as works of architecture can be interesting, but no building is 'an island, entire of itself'. Visits to houses are always more enjoyable and interesting, if we can also understand something of the personal reasons behind their construction. Like all buildings, gentry houses did not arise spontaneously, but were the result of the ideas and the hard work of many men and women. Most gentry houses are today no more than the often beautiful shells of a more or less extinct society, but they still embody the aspirations of their builders to impress their contemporaries. Those people were as alive as we are, when they saw their houses, firstly in their mind's eye, and then when they were brand new. For them their houses were not part of the national heritage, but their family's pride and joy, designed by men whom they regarded as 'contemporary architects'. What did they see through their eyes and minds? Many of the ideas which motivated them challenge our present assumptions, but that hardly matters: one can be moved by the beauties of a cathedral without sharing the faith of its medieval bishops and their craftsmen. This is, however, a book on architecture, not on social history.

Architecture is the most utilitarian of the arts – it is less about designing façades than using structures to enclose space conveniently and elegantly for human activities. In the first easily available English book with advice on building a country house – *The Elements of Architecture,* published in 1624 – the author, Sir Henry Wotton, spells out on the very first page his view (which I share) that, if a building is to have lasting value and interest as a work of architecture (rather than just be a building) it must have what he called Commodity, Firmness and Delight; we might say Convenience, Sound Construction and Attractive Appearance – appealing to the mind as well as to the eyes. Wotton was an intelligent and well-travelled man, who had been for many years the ambassador of James I to the Venetian republic. (It was he who coined the famous aphorism with its double-entendre that 'an ambassador is an honest man sent to lie abroad for the good of his country' – by which the king was not amused.) In his book he was putting into English the Latin words – *utilitas, firmitas* and *venustas* – used by the Roman architect, Vitruvius, who lived just before the time of Christ. In 1624 most educated men and women believed that Roman buildings offered the best models to emulate, and so, since Vitruvius' book on architecture was the only one to survive from his time, it long enjoyed the status of being the major authority on architecture. Few people now follow Roman models, but in my view Commodity, Firmness and Delight (despite their quaint and old-fashioned sound) still offer good headings for a study of architecture.

It is not by chance that Vitruvius and Wotton put Commodity first. If a building does not look well, people will not give it a second glance. However, if it had not been convenient, reflecting the wishes of its first owners, it would probably not have been built at all. It is no different now. When we are looking for a house to buy or rent, most of us are more concerned with convenience – with factors like the internal layout, room sizes and efficient heating – than with more superficial factors like decorative details and window shapes, which can often be changed. Delight is important, but is normally trumped by Commodity.

However, when we are visitors to houses, our priorities are often reversed, and most of us put Delight first. We are more interested in the pleasure which a building gives to our eyes and minds, than in its convenience to the people who had it built. Despite this, I believe that understanding the builders' wishes can help us to appreciate better not only the ways their houses worked as places to live in, but also the form and size, and relative positions, of the rooms themselves. And so I shall look first at most houses in terms of their Commodity – but I have only tried to deal with houses which, to me, have Delight.

If, though, a convenient and attractive house had not also been well built, it would not have survived until now. I accept that not many people are particularly interested in the way old buildings were constructed, but, having spent half my life on the fringes of the building industry, I am one of them. I have therefore written a final chapter, as an appendix, on Firmness, on the building processes, materials and technologies, by which houses with Commodity and Delight were created before the twentieth century.

I have interrupted my story after the chapter on the seventeenth century, to insert chapter four on the all-important subject of money – to try to answer the question: how were these buildings paid for? The simple answer is that most of them were financed very largely from the profits derived from the ownership of landed estates. I have therefore tried to explain how these estates were created and managed at the time of the gentry's heyday – between the 'Glorious Revolution' of 1688, when major landowners seized control of the state from the king, and the 'great' Reform Act of 1832, which marked the beginning of the end of the political predominance of the 'landed interest'. Between those dates, and largely because of the power enjoyed by landowners, most of what I regard as the finest gentry houses were built.

A history book must deal in dates, but these can never be more than approximate, even in well-documented cases. It takes time for a commission to be translated into a design, which then has to be approved; and after that craftsmen and materials have to be found and contracts signed. Only then can work begin on site. Until fairly recently little building work could be done in the winter, and a major scheme would take three or four years to complete. Which date shall one choose? I have normally followed the convention by which the date of a building is the date of its completion – when it could be used as its builder intended. I have taken my dates from the supremely authoritative recent revisions of Nikolaus Pevsner's *Buildings of England* architectural guides to Lancashire (published in 2004, 2007 and 2009), to Cumbria (2010), and to Cheshire (forthcoming). For this reason I have not given a reference for each date or designer. I have, however, added at the end of each chapter the names of a few more books which are worth reading for further information or wider background comment.

The 'centuries', which I have used in most chapter headings, do, I believe, make sensible divisions of the story, provided that you accept that the dates of my centuries do not begin or end with two noughts.

The need to make visitors' routes work smoothly means often that rooms are not seen in a way which reflects their original position or the development of the house. And so, as well as describing, with some analysis, things which a visitor may see, I have also tried to explain enough of their background – some of the 'whys?' and 'hows?', as well as the 'whats?' and 'whens?'. My hope is to make your future visits, anywhere, interesting and pleasurable – not just 'one damn room after another', as Anon once memorably said. In brief, I have tried to write the sort of book which I would have found useful some forty years ago, when I first became attracted by country houses.

In the introduction to most chapters I have briefly suggested, with the luxury of hindsight, the main themes of gentry house building in a certain period; but thereafter I have tried to show buildings through their *builders'* ideas of what Commodity and Delight – convenience and attractive decoration – meant. Hindsight can be helpful, but it is in effect a form of blindness. It prevents us from seeing and understanding things as people did in the past – people who knew no more about their future than we do of ours. Owners had their houses built, not to illustrate a later historian's thesis, but to meet their contemporary needs. It might have interested them, or even flattered them, to learn that people in the future would think that a feature of their house 'foreshadowed' one in a later and, perhaps, a greater house – but this phrase has no real meaning. Indeed, it puts the cart before the horse. A feature in one building can be re-used at a future date as the starting point of a further development, but the first builders can never have known of this 'influence' in advance; they acted, as we do, with hopes but no certain knowledge of the outcome.

To get the most from an old building, we need therefore two sets of eyes or, perhaps, two 'brains' – one programmed for the twenty-first century and one for the past. I hope that this book will help you develop this second sort of brain, so that you may more fully enjoy your visits in our present to what I regard as the finest parts of Lancashire's architectural heritage.

John Champness
Lancaster, Easter Day 2011

1.1. Warton Old Rectory. The cross-passage, shown here, was the hub of the house, with its doorways at either end and, to the left, the three doorways to the service rooms; the central door leads outside, to where the kitchen stood. The hall is to the right.

CHAPTER ONE

Medieval Origins

Introduction

Hidden behind the vicarage at Warton, near Carnforth, **Warton Old Rectory** is probably the oldest house in Lancashire [1.1; 1.2]. The tall quatrefoil window in the west gable, along with the mouldings on the doorway arches, show that it dates from around the middle of the fourteenth century. Only then were members of the gentry becoming wealthy enough to afford the good building materials which would help their houses to survive. It has to be said that most visitors find the house somewhat disappointing, because it is no more than a roofless ruin; it was even subdivided into cottages in the nineteenth century. However, these later changes have been pared away, and so it now gives a fairly clear picture of its original structure and thus some insight into the housing needs of the family for whom it was built – and, by extension, of most gentry families in the Middle Ages, and later. Warton Old Rectory can be thought of as the seed from which all the splendours of gentry houses in Lancashire were later to develop.

Builders

Ever since agriculture, rather than hunting and gathering, became the most important means of food-production, there must always have been a 'landed gentry' in the sense of people who laid claim – and could support that claim by force if necessary – to the ownership or control of sizeable areas of land and consequently to political power at the local level. There must, therefore, always have been 'gentry houses', but the earliest which survive in a recognisable form above the ground in Lancashire, and with a few exceptions in other parts of England too (like the old hall at Burton Agnes, Yorkshire, which dates from the 1170s, and the so-called Stokesay Castle, Shropshire, which was largely built in the 1280s) date from the fourteenth century. By then they were the products of a long evolution. Gentlemen in the Middle Ages built houses more or less as their parents and grandparents had done – in what is now called the 'vernacular tradition' – and they must have discussed the advantages and drawbacks associated with each slight change made. If

1.2. Warton Old Rectory, seen from the back. The doorway of the cross-passage is in the centre, the gable of the hall to the left, and the doorway into the house from the kitchen to the right. Behind the house is what is probably the window of the former chapel.

they had friends outside their immediate locality, they had a greater variety of small changes to discuss and, occasionally, to adopt – thus leading to the slow evolution of gentry house design. House builders in any age tend to fall into three rough groups: there is a small minority of people for whom the old ways are always the best, and then a smaller minority who are eager to accept whatever is new; but the majority are conservatives, who favour traditional ways, but accept a few minor changes. Moreover, the building industry has always been conservative, and, until the rise of professional architects in the seventeenth and eighteenth centuries, all buildings were designed by the men who went on to construct them; these craftsmen were naturally reluctant to design something which they had not built previously, since a failure in a house would also lead to the collapse of their career.

Over the six hundred years which this short book spans, the gentry changed greatly – the heyday of their political power and wealth was the 'long eighteenth century' between 1688 and 1832 – but some of their attributes and attitudes remained fairly constant. Members of the gentry were always very conscious of their status – believing that they were called by God to exercise power and stressing their pedigree whenever they could. They expected deference and obedience from the other members of their community, but few had any ambition to play a rôle on a stage above the level of the county.

They were, basically, the holders or owners of middle-sized estates, or manors – no more than around 2000 acres, or 800 hectares, of land (which correspond to eight square kilometres, or eight of the grid squares on an Ordnance Survey Landranger map). This is a large but not a vast area, but land was the commodity which counted above all else. Their estates were all-important, so that the head of any family had a duty to maintain the estate intact and to pass it on to the next generation. The reason was simple: landownership was the foundation of the gentry's claim to lead society. Until the 'Industrial Revolution' in the eighteenth century the land, through agriculture, animal husbandry and the mining of the subsoil, gave the nation most of its food, drink and raw materials, and provided employment for most of the population. From these consequences the holders of the land derived their right to govern, both locally and nationally, and almost no-one disputed the claim until the eighteenth century. For centuries, an income from land conferred higher social status than one from any other source; furthermore, this income was not merely stable but tended to rise thanks to the country's slow economic expansion.

Until the Industrial Revolution, when it became a world-leader, Lancashire was a relatively poor county.[1] Its most productive soils, which provided the money to pay for the building and maintenance of gentry houses, were concentrated in about half of its area, lying between the high moorlands to the east and the low-lying mosslands (or fens) to the west – more specifically, in the valleys of the Mersey, the Douglas, the Ribble, the Wyre , the Lune and the Kent, plus the narrow corridor along the western fringes of the Bowland and Rossendale massifs, now roughly marked on a map by the M6 motorway and the West Coast railway line. This lack of good land, coupled with the fact that the Crown, and from 1485 the Earl of Derby, owned much of it, meant that there were few major gentlemen in Lancashire. There were, though, plenty of middling gentlemen, and some of them built significant houses for their family to live in and to display their gentry status. These are the houses with which this book is concerned.

Commodity

The housing needs of a gentry family

What would have been the requirements for a gentleman's house – it was often called his seat – in the fourteenth century? There were several. As well as providing private accommodation for his personal family and their household servants – who were regarded as his extended family – it would have had to provide space for the communal centre of the life of a manor. Each gentry house was the centre of arrangements which we, not they, call the 'feudal system' and which was well established when Warton Old Rectory was built. Briefly, since 1066 all the land in England belonged to the king, who kept much for himself but granted the rest to a few score tenants-in-chief, who held it in return for serving him. In their turn they granted some of their lands, in exchange for services promised, to lesser men – and so on down to the level of the individual manor, at which some degree of protection and the right to farm small parcels of land were granted by a gentleman to his tenants in return for their service as agricultural labourers on his estate.

No less importantly in a society where few people could read, a gentleman's seat would have to demonstrate his status clearly – by being large and impressive, by flaunting all the latest status symbols plus an adequate provision of the security-measures necessary in an unpoliced society and, not least, by displaying his family's coat of arms. Lastly, if his manor house were at some distance from the parish church – as was the case in much of the North West, where parishes were large and contained several townships or settlements – a gentleman might seek the bishop's permission to build a private chapel where Mass might be celebrated. He would hope thereby to secure for his household and tenantry some comfort and strength to bear the trials and tribulations of their life, which was almost entirely dependent on subsistence agriculture and therefore at the mercy of the local weather – with no help from the outside world.

Almost all of this can be seen at **Warton Old Rectory**. The plan [1.3] shows that visitors enter the simple barn-like building from the north, and that there is another door opposite them; the space between the two is normally called the 'cross-passage'. Turning to the right, visitors find themselves in the hall, which was an impressive space – it measures about 13 metres by 8, and is 9 metres high – because it was the heart and hub of the house. It was always heated and was the room to which almost everyone went first. It was the administrative centre of the family's estate – the room where the manor court sat (to organise the farming of the land as well as punish minor offenders) and where the community's main entertainments took place. We need only a little imagination to picture it

1.3. Warton Old Rectory. The normal medieval plan with (from right to left) the open-roofed hall, divided by the cross-passage from the two-storey 'lower' end with its service rooms and passage to the outside kitchen; above these rooms was the family's chamber. The walls are very thick, because they are largely built of rubble stonework.

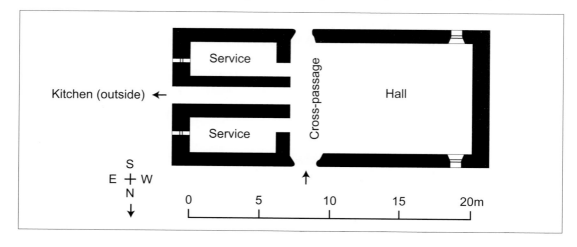

open to the rafters of its steeply pitched (and, therefore, probably thatched) roof. There is no sign of a fireplace in any of the walls, so the room must have been heated by a fire on an open hearth in the middle of the floor; this was the normal practice in the fourteenth century, even in the houses of the gentry. The smoke would have found its way out through a sort of wooden chimney, called a 'louvre', built between the rafters. At night the fire would have been covered by a domed lid called a 'couvre-feu' (the origin of our word 'curfew') in the hope that some embers would survive to be revived on the following morning. (There is a good example of a louvre – which was taken down from the roof in 1950 – at Gainsborough Old Hall in Lincolnshire.)

By our standards, with draughts from the front and back doors and from the few but probably unglazed windows, this would not have been a comfortable room, but by the criteria of most medieval Lancastrians it was luxurious. Second only to a large retinue of servants and men-at-arms, a high and spacious hall was the most potent status symbol in the Middle Ages. When it was built, probably in the 1340s, this hall was almost certainly bigger than the nave of the parish church and would have impressed people for miles around.

At meal times the lord, his family and their guests sat on a dais at the far (or 'upper') end of the hall, away from the draughts near the entrance doors. Their retainers and the servants of guests sat at tables along the side walls. (At night many of them slept on the floor, made of rammed earth under layers of rushes – in more comfort than in most people's homes.) All the tables were boards on trestles and, except at meal times, they and the benches would have been ranged flat around the side walls to clear as much space as possible around the potentially dangerous open hearth.

At the 'lower' end of the hall, in the wall beside the cross-passage, there are three identical doorways [1.1]. The central one leads to a corridor and through a door to the yard outside, where the kitchen was built separately to reduce the risk of fire. The others give access to rooms which were storerooms for food and drink – now known, respectively, as the pantry and the buttery. Outside the 'back door' of the cross-passage there was a staircase leading to a chamber on the upper floor above the storerooms; this was the family's bed-sitting room which may have had a fireplace and would have provided a degree of privacy and some space where close friends or important visitors could be received. Here the floor would have been of timber boards, and the walls would probably have been plastered and then, possibly, decorated with woven or painted hangings. There would have been a double bed with curtains, a chest or two for clothes and precious possessions, and a few stools.

The Old Rectory provides a good example of what might be called the normal plan and cross-section of a medieval manor house – the public open hall, then the cross-passage and lastly a two-storey section containing storage rooms below the lord's private chamber. It was, however, merely the largest among a jumble of other buildings on the site. It is thought, for example, that the two-light window in the present vicarage, behind the gable of the hall, was part of the Rectory's chapel. Until the late fifteenth century it was rare for gentry houses to be designed and built to one integrated plan; they were simply developed according to the changing circumstances and private needs of families. A new building had to be tucked in where it was least inconvenient, and most people had to live on the site, while a new hall or kitchen or stable was being built.

Security

The lord of a manor was significantly wealthier than the other members of his local community and must have felt the need to take measures to increase the security of his house. One thing which we cannot now see easily at Warton is some provision for defence, but there are a few hints. The house was built of stone, with the local limestone used as rubble in the metre-thick walls, and the less local, but more easily carved, sandstone serving for the surrounds to windows and doors. Stone had the highest status of all building materials and was also used because of the greater protection which it gave. In North-West England in the later Middle Ages what people feared most was a repeat of the highly damaging incursion by the Scots army which reached Preston in 1322. Hints of this fear can be seen in the tiny ground-floor windows of the buttery and pantry.

Every gentry house must have had, at least, a timber palisade around it; those in the lower-lying areas probably had a moat as well, which would have provided a supply of drinking water and fish, and a rudimentary means of sewage disposal. (This arrangement can be well seen at Little Moreton Hall in Cheshire, where the privies empty directly into the moat.) There are some 70 formerly moated sites recorded in Lancashire. A map and a painting show that there was a moat at Ordsall Hall in the mid-nineteenth century.[2] Speke Hall has a moat (now dry) on three sides, and there is still a wet moat hidden in the private grounds of Thurland Castle and of Arley Hall, now the home of the Wigan Golf Club. More accessible, but less attractive, are the remains of the moat around the house in Clayton Park, Manchester.

Those gentry families who could afford to build defences in stone had two choices. They could, firstly, replace a timber palisade with a stone wall and, when appropriate, rebuild their house within the defensive perimeter. Such a wall can be glimpsed from the A6 at **Beetham Hall Farm**, a private house near Milnthorpe, where it part-surrounds a large

1.4. Middleton Hall. Behind the arch of the two-storey gatehouse stands the main house, with the doorway leading to the cross-passage and, on its right, the hall window.

but ruined mid-fourteenth-century house, now used as a barn. A finer, early-fifteenth-century, example, where the gateway in the high wall can still be seen from the A683, is at **Middleton Hall Farm**, a private house near Sedbergh [1.4]. The doors of houses and gateways were always closed and barred before nightfall; after then the normal way in, if entry were allowed, would be through a narrow wicket door, opened by the porter, such as one can see in many Oxbridge colleges, and at **Smithills Hall**, near Bolton.

Alternatively, gentlemen could build a thick-walled tower – more often than not attached to the upper end of the hall, for the convenience of their family. This might have been more expensive, but would have provided greater protection under attack, even while being built, and would have been easier to defend with fewer people. It would also have stood out more proudly in the landscape, thus providing display as well as defence. The finest surviving medieval tower in Lancashire, built soon after the Scottish incursion, is at **Ashton Hall** [1.5]. Now the home of the Lancaster Golf Club, it is private, but is visible from the A588. Its walls, which are 2 metres thick, are built of large irregular blocks of sandstone and rise some 15 metres, with turrets placed diagonally at each corner. The tower has two storeys above a vaulted basement, but nothing else of the original internal arrangements survives, and the windows are Georgian sashes. Other such towers are visible at **Borwick Hall, Towneley Hall** and **Turton Tower**, where they form the core around which a larger house grew later. Similar ones were built all over Cumbria, where the risk of Scottish marauders was greater than in Lancashire, and the best surviving example, with its attached hall, is at the private **Yanwath Hall Farm**, near Penrith.

Whatever form of physical security the lord of a manor chose, it was always supplemented by a small contingent of menservants, sometimes in a sort of livery, who were a living, active status symbol. They had a double purpose, since they could be used not merely for passive defence, but for active offence in defence of their master's interests – to intimidate neighbours and overawe judges. Not until Victorian times was being a gentleman regarded more as a matter of behaviour than of landowning and of power; and a few gentlemen disagreed even then.

More family accommodation

Warton Old Rectory, however interesting, is only a roofless shell, and so a better building to give the feel of the shape and the internal space of a gentry house of the same period is **Smithills Hall**, Bolton, which stands at the junction of two steep-sided small valleys. The oldest part, the hall, was probably built about 1350 by William Radclyffe, a member of a significant family of landowners north of Manchester. It is a little smaller than the one at Warton; its outer walls appear to have been built of stone originally, but the internal walls were timber-framed [1.6]. (A comparable building of about 1420 is the hall at **Samlesbury Hall**, which is now an antiques showroom. The hall has the added interest of being constructed of cruck trusses – see the Appendix on Firmness – but it was much mishandled in Victorian times. Its screen, which must originally have stood at the lower end of the hall, was chopped about and placed at the upper end, by the bay window – so that, sadly, it gives a seriously wrong impression of a medieval hall.)

1.5. Ashton Hall. The windows are Georgian, but the structure of the tower dates from *c*.1340.

The lower end of the house at Smithills has been modified, and visitors now enter the hall not through the main door (which still has its wicket) but through the central passage from the kitchen area. Above the centre of the now-flagged floor are two closely spaced arch-like timber roof-trusses; these must have supported the louvre above the central hearth. At either end of the hall there are two more pairs of closely spaced trusses. Those at the lower end are related to what is called a spere-truss, in which tall posts, set about a metre inside the main walls, rise to the tie-beam below the rafters; they support a sort of draught-screen in front of the main doorways and also carry a tall arch which defines the cross-passage.

Spere trusses are a feature of a number of halls in Lancashire and Cheshire. It is generally thought that they are vestiges of the two rows of

1.6. Smithills Hall: the interior of the open-roofed hall. Beyond the site of the original fire is the upper end wall, behind which is the two-storey cross-wing containing the family's parlour on the ground floor and its chamber above.

posts which had been used to support the roofs of the earliest form of major timber-framed halls – now called 'aisled halls' – and that, even though better carpentry techniques later made such posts unnecessary, a pair were normally retained at the lower end of halls, because of their value in creating a draught-screen. When seen from the lord's table at the upper end of the hall, their tall arch also has the important – aesthetic and therefore social – advantage, clearly visible at **Ordsall**, of emphasising the height of the hall [1.7].

At the upper end of the hall at Smithills a similar narrower space between two roof-trusses marks the site of the dais where the lord's table stood. To the right of the end wall a doorway leads into the family's parlour (or living room) and from there to the chamber above. The plank-like vertical posts and horizontal rails of the end walls are braced by timbers which form decorative patterns, rather like the quatrefoil window in the end wall at Warton. Similarly shaped wind-braces (which prevent the roof from leaning under the pressure of the wind) can be seen between the rafters and the horizontal timbers, called purlins, of the roof.

The rooms for the family's private use and daily living – which at Warton had been above the service rooms at the lower end of the hall – are now at Smithills beyond the upper end of the hall, in a separately framed cross-wing. This was added to the original house, probably around 1500, and its rooms must have superseded earlier rooms at the lower end. (Building a cross-wing, rather than merely extending the hall lengthwise, allowed more space to be provided conveniently close to the upper end of the hall, and cross-wings with two storeys soon became a standard feature of gentry houses.) These two family rooms have, on both floors, fireplaces in the middle of what was originally their outside wall. The parlour is fairly low under its heavily moulded ceiling beams, but the more spacious chamber above has a fine open roof carried on a pair of tie-beams: it forms a sort of mini-hall, where the owner could entertain special guests in some splendour. The importance of these rooms is shown outside by their prominent gable, but the lower end of the hall has been rebuilt. The only building, therefore, in our area to give some idea of the outward appearance of a late-medieval gentry house with a central hall and two gabled cross-wings is what is now called the **Castle Dairy Restaurant** in Kendal, which was probably the dower house of the family who occupied the castle. However, its interior has been altered and it has also gained four impressive, but later, chimneystacks. There is, though, a good picture of such a house in the background of a painting of Astley Hall, which is displayed at Astley Hall itself [3.1].

1.7. Ordsall Hall: a drawing (dated 1883) of the spere truss, whose arch is 6m tall; behind this was the cross-passage.

It is clear from such poems as the Anglo-Saxon *Beowulf* or *Sir Gawain and the Green Knight*, which dates from the mid-fourteenth century, that the normal medieval custom was to entertain honoured guests in the hall. However, by about 1380, when William Langland was writing his long alliterative poem, *Piers the Ploughman,* the tendency was growing (at least in the South and Midlands) for the lord of the manor and his close family to eat most of their meals in their parlour, and only to eat in the hall on particularly important occasions. Langland criticised this shunning of the society of the hall as a lack of Christian humility among contemporary lords.

> Wretched is the hall. Each day in the week
> There the lord and lady liketh not to sit.
> Now have the rich a rule to eat by themselves
> In a privy parlour, *for poor men's sakes,*
>   [i.e. because of the poor men – to get away from them]
> Or in a chamber with a chimney, and leave the chief hall,
> That was made for meals, *for men to eat in.*[3]
>   [i.e. 'common' men or servants, not gentlemen]

Langland saw this as a sign of the break-up of the traditional society, but it was in part a consequence of the customary obligation of a gentleman to be a generous host. The same thing was happening in monasteries, where abbots, important men who had originally lived alongside their monks, were having special lodgings built where they could entertain high-ranking visitors or discuss confidential matters; or just enjoy the pleasure of privacy. By Tudor times such a practice was also common among the gentry in the North. Lords and their families sought greater privacy within the communal house, and private rooms for the entertainment of special guests became more and more important. The word 'family', which once had meant 'household', was coming to be used in its narrower modern sense. Moralists bewailed this process, but it was to underlie the development of gentry houses and culminated in the nineteenth century.

A good impression of the last stage in the evolution of medieval gentry houses is given by the hall at **Ordsall Hall** in Salford, which was built in 1512 to replace an older hall by Sir Alexander Radclyffe. He was related to the Radclyffes of Smithills and was one of the most prominent men in the county. His new hall is a little larger and taller than the one at Smithills and was built so that its upper end connected with a two-storey, timber-framed private wing, which had been built around 1360.[4] At the lower end it has the three service doors off the cross passage, a tall spere truss with tracery above it. [1.7] The windows on one side are small and placed only at the top of the wall. There was originally a similar arrangement on the other side, so that the room would have been somewhat darker than now.

There is no 'perfect example' of a late-medieval gentry house in Lancashire, but the next-best thing is **Rufford Old Hall** [1.8], which was built as a new house, probably around 1530, by Sir Robert Hesketh, whose long-established family was second in importance in the area only to the Stanleys, the family led by the Earl of Derby. The house lost its

1.8. Rufford Old Hall. Only the original hall of c.1530 with its bay window survives; the upper-end cross-wing (to the right) was removed c.1720, and the lower-end cross-wing was replaced in 1724 by one brought from Holmeswood Hall.

original upper-end cross-wing on the right (as visitors approach) around 1720, and in 1724 gained a cross-wing on the left from Holmeswood Hall, another house belonging to the Hesketh family. However, the hall itself is the largest in Lancashire and dominates the house. It is one of the finest of its date still existing in England and also contains the finest collection of late-medieval status symbols in any Lancashire house.

Delight

At **Rufford** visitors now enter the hall, not through the original front door with its pair of dragons in the lintel, but from the lower-end cross-wing – as at Smithills. They pass under the spere truss with its massive traceried posts, and around the heavily carved and panelled screen with its grotesquely carved pinnacles [1.9]. This is not part of the hall's structure, but was probably placed there to hide from the lord's table the comings and goings in the cross-passage. There is a similar, much simpler, screen in the hall of **Chetham's Hospital** in Manchester (which was originally the home of a college of priests who worshipped in what is now Manchester Cathedral). On the other side of the cross-passage at Rufford one can see the doors to the original service rooms (and staircase) and, on some of the timbers, the marks which the carpenters made in their yard to ensure that the frame was correctly put together. (See the Appendix on Firmness.)

The hall has a high open roof, in which five 'hammer-beams', projecting horizontally into the hall, carry arches supporting an upper beam – a 'collar' – which spans between the principal rafters. Such a truss was regarded, then as now, as the finest form of timber roof and therefore the one which reflected the greatest glory on the owner of the house. On the end of each hammer beam is an angel carrying a shield; however, they are not all of the same pattern and are not mentioned in the building accounts and were probably brought later from elsewhere, perhaps from the church of a monastery.[5] The shields may well have been painted with the coat of arms of the Hesketh family – to form a link

1.9. Rufford Old Hall. A drawing, dated 1884, showing the hall roof, with its hammer beams and their angels, the spere truss and screen, and two doors in the wall beyond leading to service rooms.

F Hooper

with those carved on the collars of the trusses, which show the arms of a few of the important families with whom the Heskeths had intermarried. During all of the period covered by this book it was important for a gentry family to display a long pedigree and a wide-ranging kinship, both to stress their personal importance and to bolster, through their mutual obligations, the stability of the society in which they played a leading rôle. Entertaining guests at home, and being entertained elsewhere, were among the most important parts of the life of a gentleman and his family.

The next status symbol, which a medieval visitor would have noticed after the roof, was the fireplace, safely situated in the left-hand wall, out of the way but clearly visible. And then he would have noticed the tall, five-sided bay-window, which is – and was – the most striking of all the late-medieval status symbols [1.8 and 1.10]. He would probably have seen it already, since such features were almost always built on the side of the house from which it was normally approached by the people who mattered. (Samlesbury Hall and Ordsall Hall have comparable bay windows, and Ordsall even has two – one of 1512 in the hall, and one built sometime after 1600, when the family wing was extended at the lower end of the hall.) An interesting feature of the bay-window at Rufford is that it displays inside two motifs – the eagle's claw and the three legs of Man – which were emblems of the Stanleys. This would have been understood then as meaning that the Heskeths wanted to show in their seat that they were in the service of the Earl of Derby. To do this conferred status on the Heskeths, and the Earl, in his turn, would have been flattered by their recognition of his preeminence.

1.10. Rufford Old Hall. A drawing of 1884, showing the upper end of the hall with the canopy over the lord's table, two doorways into the family wing, and the inside of the bay window.

There is very little furniture at Rufford, but that would have been normal. Fixed tables were not introduced into halls until Elizabethan times, and only the lord had a chair; until the seventeenth century other people sat on benches. The lord's table would have stood on a dais at the upper end [1.10], connected by a pair of doorways to his private rooms. These have disappeared, though the doorways are visible, and something of what might have been there can be seen in the high quality timberwork from the family's cross-wing from Holmeswood

Hall which is now at the *lower* end at Rufford. In contrast to the gloom of the hall, the dais would have been bathed in light from the bay-window and placed under the coved canopy which emphasised his status. There is a similar canopy at **Chetham's Hospital**, but the finest example in the country is at **Adlington Hall**, in Cheshire. This is dated 1505 and has five rows of panels, still painted with the coats of arms of the many families to whom the Leghs of Adlington were related.

The main purpose of the dais was to raise the lord's table symbolically above the level of the others in the hall and also to avoid the need for the family to tread on the floor of the hall itself. This was sometimes nicknamed 'the marsh'; and we can understand why from this – probably more humorous than serious – complaint (written originally in Latin to Cardinal Wolsey's physician) by the great Dutch scholar, Erasmus, who lived in England between 1509 and 1514:

> 'The floor is of clay, strewn with rushes; these are often renewed, but under them there lies, for up to twenty years, an undisturbed base, made of spittle, vomit, dogs' and men's urine, spilt beer, bits of fish and many things too nasty to mention.'[6]

There may well have been some truth in these words – Cardinal Wolsey is said to have carried a sweet-smelling pomander in front of his nose, whenever he had to go into the hall at Hampton Court – but they also reflect what Erasmus' gentry friends would have regarded as a truism – that, although God might regard all people's souls as having equal value, gentlemen were superior to other men in all other ways. With Langland's lament in *Piers the Ploughman* they provide literary evidence that, as the Middle Ages wore on, gentry families sought more privacy and comfort and also finer reception rooms. This wish was the main motor for all the changes to be described in the following chapters.

One related development which cannot be seen in the fabric of medieval gentry houses, though it is clear in later ones, was the separation of the family's entrance from the servants' entrance. It would be impossible to prove, but the custom must have grown whereby the family used the 'front door' of the cross-passage, while servants and people delivering food or fuel used the back door – which would have led from a farmyard rather than from a well-swept and tidy courtyard. The twain might occasionally have met at the lower end of the hall, but would not have used the same door.

References

1. This statement, which may offend many Lancastrians, represents the consensus opinion of all recent Lancashire historians. J. K. Walton's view is typical: 'By all available measures Lancashire was one of the poorest of English counties in the early sixteenth century. Indeed, it had long been so, and was to remain so for well over a century.' J. K. Walton, *Lancashire: A Social History 1558–1939* (1987), p. 8.

2. A plan of 1849 (opposite p. 214 of volume IV of the *Victoria County History of Lancashire*) shows a moat surrounding the house. There is a water colour of *c.*1820 showing the moat in the City of Salford Museum and Art Gallery. Anthony Blacklay (*pers. comm.*).

3. W. Langland, *Piers the Ploughman*, text B, passus X, lines 97–101, (quoted in M. Girouard, *Life in the English Country House* (1978), p.30).

4. It is rare to be able to date medieval houses accurately, since there is seldom any reliable documentary evidence for them. We have therefore to compare the many buildings, whose dates are unknown, with the very few whose dates are certain — a process which can generate as much heat as light. The modern science of dendrochronology — which involves analysis of the relative thickness of the 'tree rings' in timber beams — can, however, almost always provide a reliable way of dating a building by calculating the 'felling-dates' of the trees which form its beams. The process is fairly expensive, but it was used to date these buildings at Ordsall.

5. Richard Dean (*pers. comm.*).

6. The slightly longer Latin text is in N. Lloyd, *History of the English House* (1975), p. 80.

2.1. Stonyhurst: The gatehouse tower of *c*.1592 was a symbol of the owner's political power and of his Classical education: its columns are placed in the correct Roman order – from bottom to top: Doric, Ionic, Corinthian and Composite. The cupolas at the back of the tower were not added, however, until 1712.

CHAPTER TWO

Gentry Houses in the Sixteenth Century

Introduction

In the 1530s Robert Hesketh must have felt that in Rufford, with its high open hall, framed by the two gables of its two-storeyed cross-wings, he had an imposing house which would display his family's rank for many years to come. However, his seat was already old-fashioned by the standards of the Home Counties, and within a generation or so would be regarded as small and outmoded in Lancashire as well, thanks to the unrelenting pressure for better accommodation to meet newly felt needs. Houses which had once passed muster were no longer adequate for ambitious families and had to be extended to provide not only private chambers for family members but – also and more importantly – more impressive reception rooms at the upper end and, wherever possible, on the sunnier side of the building. Various experiments were tried, and the story in the sixteenth century is more complicated than in any other – hence the length of this chapter. However, no standard pattern was evolved. The hall never lost its status as the centre of the community, but in the course of the century it was replaced as the main reception room for the family's visitors by what was normally called the great chamber; and, since this was often on the first floor, a fine staircase became important. Lastly, during the reign of Queen Elizabeth, every gentry family felt that it owed it to itself to provide somehow the age's most striking status symbol, a long gallery.

Builders

Most of the builders of gentry houses in the sixteenth century were, like those in the Middle Ages, men whose ancestors had owned estates for generations and who had grown richer, thanks to the profits of agriculture and also to the dowries brought by their wives, who were sometimes also heiresses. Such men despised Queen Elizabeth's chief minister, Lord Burghley, who had come from a family of small Welsh landholders. On the other hand, he repaid their disdain, when he said that gentry status was nothing more than 'ancient riches'.[1] He was right, but he was, at the same time, also amassing the fortune from the public purse which was 'ancient' by the time that his sons were ennobled by James I in 1605 as the Earls of Salisbury and of Exeter.

A number of gentlemen in the mid-sixteenth century were able to help their family fortunes by taking advantage of the Dissolution of the Monasteries, when estates, formerly owned by monastic communities, suddenly became available. In 1536–40, Henry VIII confiscated all of the land which had belonged to the monasteries – at least a fifth of the acreage of England – as well as their buildings and worldly goods. Being always short of money, he and his son, Edward VI, sold off about three-quarters of this land during the next ten or fifteen years; and since land was, economically and above all socially, the most valuable of all purchasable goods, anybody with ready money – gentleman or not and, probably, Catholic or not – wanted to invest it in buying some. (When Henry's elder daughter, the strongly Catholic Queen Mary, tried to reverse the process, she failed.) These monastic estates were sold as going agricultural concerns, mainly at first in large parcels to people who wanted to sell them on, but often to people who already had an interest in certain properties. They were not sold off cheaply, as is sometimes claimed: most were sold at a price equivalent to 20 years' rent – the normal market rate.

There was obviously some sharp practice, and some gentlemen were well placed, thanks to connections with the Court or the government, to buy cheaply by avoiding the open market. The site and local estates of Furness Abbey were sold in 1540 to Sir Thomas Curwen, the most important landowner in West Cumberland. He passed some of them on as a dowry to his son-in-law, John Preston of Holker, thus helping to establish that family. The third Earl of Derby, who was one of the king's commissioners for the confiscation of monastic lands, bought the site and local estates of Burscough Priory, where his ancestors were buried, but, having reburied them in Ormskirk parish church, he sold off much of the land. Some of his associates prospered more. His nephew, Lord Monteagle of Hornby Castle, was able to buy the lands of Hornby Priory and also of Conishead Priory, but he sold the latter on. More egregious was one of his agents, Thomas Holcroft, who bought the estates belonging to Lytham Priory and Cartmel Priory, and also those owned by the friaries at Lancaster, Preston and Warrington. He also acquired Vale Royal Abbey in Cheshire, where he built himself a family seat. His son sold Lytham in 1597 to Sir Richard Molyneux of Sefton, who sold it on to Cuthbert Clifton in 1606 and thereby helped to augment that family's fortunes.

Towards the end of the sixteenth century a number of the builders of houses were newly rich men who, by purchasing estates, aimed to establish their gentry status and doubtless hoped to found a dynasty. Borwick Hall was enlarged by a Kendal cloth merchant, Robert Bindloss, in the 1590s, and Hough End Hall was built in 1596 by Nicholas Mosley, a Manchester merchant. Richard Shuttleworth, whose grandson of the same name inherited Gawthorpe Hall in 1608, had been a judge, and so was Sir Thomas Walmesley, who built Hacking Hall in 1607.

The gentry was never a rigid caste. To a large extent it was self-defining. In 1577 William Harrison, in his *A Description of England*, wrote that any man who owned land and 'can live without manual labour and thereto [= in addition] will bear the port, charge and countenance' of a gentleman, could call himself one. By these three words he meant that a man should display generosity, hospitality, courage, panache and, not least, a willingness to play a leading role in local society – notably as one of the Justices of the Peace. (In their quarterly meetings, the JPs in Quarter Sessions dealt with minor crimes and until 1889 provided the local government of the county.) Harrison added, 'He shall for money have a coat of arms bestowed upon him by the Heralds [of the College of Arms] and be reputed a gentleman for ever after'.

Harrison might have added that a man's claim to gentry status would only be valid in practice, if it were accepted as well by the other members of the 'County élite' of acknowledged local gentlemen. This was much more important; it was they who vetted a man's wealth and behaviour and then commissioned him to serve with them in what was a sort of hereditary officer class, destined by birth to live in a house on a certain site, to be an unchallenged leader of local society, to exercise considerable influence in County affairs and sometimes to represent the County in Parliament. Landownership brought status but entailed obligations. All through the period covered in this book the ideal of *'noblesse oblige'* was the object of lip-service, and it was often put into practice. The Victorian historian, Thomas Macaulay, put it trenchantly when he wrote that gentlemen 'had the virtues and vices which flourish among men set from their birth in high places and accustomed to authority, to observance and self-respect'.[2]

Commodity

More reception rooms in wings

Probably the earliest rooms in Lancashire, built as an extension specifically to entertain important visitors outside the family's chamber, are at **Smithills Hall**. [2.2] The estate had come to John Barton around 1485 on his marriage to his cousin, the heiress Cecily Radcliffe, and it was probably he who built the cross-wing at the upper end of the hall,

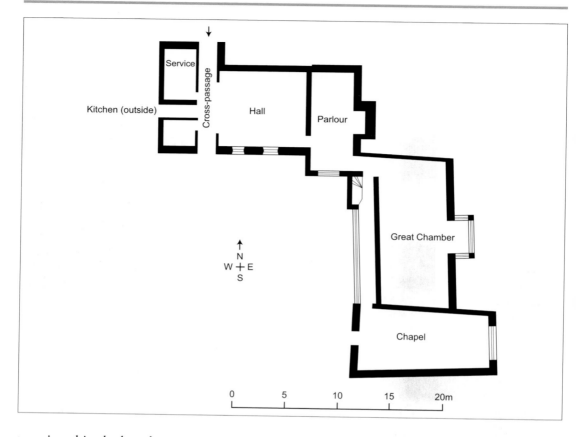

mentioned in the last chapter. In 1516 his son, Andrew Barton, also made a good marriage – to Agnes Stanley of Hooton, near Chester – and doubtless wanted to stamp his mark on the house as well. Probably in the 1520s he built the long, two-storey, timber-framed wing between his father's cross-wing and the house's chapel [2.3]. (The core of the larger, much rebuilt wing on the other side of the courtyard was added somewhat later to create a balanced design.) The upper floor of Barton's wing was divided into chambers, reached by a separately-built corridor – a feature which was fairly common already in aristocratic houses, but new at the level of the gentry, and which was also to be used at Speke Hall a generation later. The lower room, which was probably called the great chamber although it is unlikely to have contained a bed, was used for formal dining and entertaining. It is a spacious room – almost as large as the hall and with a large square bay window; it has richly moulded ceiling beams and contemporary panelling, but it is rather low.

Panelling, replacing hangings, was a new status symbol in the sixteenth century and became popular as a way of making rooms feel less chilly by making the walls slightly warmer to the touch. (When first fitted, all panelling would have appeared lighter in colour than it does now; much

2.2. Smithills Hall: the plan showing how the original hall with its service rooms to the left of the cross-passage was extended c.1500 by an upper-end cross-wing containing the family's parlour (and chamber above) and then, in the 1520s, by a longer wing between the house and the chapel, containing the great chamber (with chambers above).

2.3. Smithills Hall: from left to right the roof of the hall, the gable of the cross-wing, and the two-storeyed wing built in the 1520s.

2.4. Smithills Hall: linenfold and Romayne work in the panelling of the great chamber, built in the 1520s, showing also two emblems of the Barton family, a stag's head and an oak sprig.

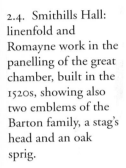

of it was stained in the nineteenth century to make it look 'antique'.) The great chamber at Smithills shows an early form, in which individual panels were decorated with the pleated motif, introduced from the Netherlands and now called 'linenfold' [2.4]. The room also contains good examples of the short-lived fashion for medallions containing profiles in bas-relief; they may represent Andrew Barton and his wife, since they contain his initials and other emblems of the family. (The contemporary name of 'Romayne work' for these medallions indicates their origin in Renaissance Italy; there are more sophisticated examples at Hampton Court Palace, dating from 1521 – busts made of terra cotta which represent Roman emperors.)

Barton's example of extending his house was later followed at **Samlesbury Hall** by Sir Thomas Southworth. In

1545 he built a wing at right-angles to the upper end of the hall, to link it with the chapel – providing a ground-floor great chamber with a series of first-floor chambers which gave access to the chapel's family pew. The lower room has richly moulded ceiling beams, and the upper ones have a fine open roof. There are fireplaces on both floors, some boasting heraldic devices, and their presence is declared outside by a row of three projecting chimneystacks [2.5], one of which bears the Southworths' coat of arms. (Chimney stacks, often richly decorated and rising high above roofs, were to become a major status symbol in Elizabeth's reign – showing that the house had many fireplaces.) Outside, on the side facing the courtyard, the walls were built of elaborately decorated (and now highly restored) timber-framing with a few panels of Romayne work, but much of the other side was built of brick – perhaps its earliest use in Lancashire. This was probably done to link the chimneystacks and be strong enough to hold the fine stone, traceried windows which – tradition holds – were salvaged from Whalley Abbey after its Dissolution.

The grandest wings in the Lancashire area – two of them – were built for Walter Strickland, when he enlarged **Sizergh Castle** in the 1560s [2.6]. He started by remodelling the centre of the medieval house by placing a new hall above a service basement – perhaps the first example here of an arrangement which must have been derived from the one at a house like Warton Old Rectory, with its family room above the service rooms. (All this is now hidden behind eighteenth-century work.) He then flanked the entry courtyard with a pair of long, two-storey wings, which created at one stroke a balanced design. The wing on the left accommodated a new kitchen and other service rooms. The one on the right contained

2.5. Samlesbury Hall: the back of the wing of c.1545, showing brickwork, chimneys, and windows (perhaps) from Whalley Abbey.

2.6. Sizergh Castle:
the entrance
courtyard, showing
the tower of *c*.1350,
the (since rebuilt)
hall to its left, and
the two extended
cross-wings of *c*.1560.

two major status symbols – two-room 'lodgings' on the ground floor for important visitors (to proclaim the hospitality which Strickland, as a gentleman, felt obliged to provide) and a newly fashionable long gallery on the first floor.

Houses with courtyards

The sites at Smithills, Samlesbury and Sizergh were fairly spacious, but on those sites which were tightly constrained by a moat – and these were more common than we now think – owners who wanted to extend their houses were often forced to build wings in such a way as created a closed courtyard. The most famous such house in the North West is the timber-framed **Little Moreton Hall**, near Congleton, but **Speke Hall**, near Liverpool Airport, is also built of timber framing and is almost as fine. It was built over some sixty years by three generations of the Norris family and completed with the nearly symmetrical entrance front on the north in 1598.

In the early 1530s the recently-knighted Sir William Norris built a new full-height hall with a flat ceiling [2.7] to supersede a fourteenth-century cruck-framed hall; probably for reasons of economy this was kept but downgraded to stand among the service rooms on the other side of the cross-passage. The hall's fireplace backs onto this passage – which is rare in gentry houses, but common in farmhouses. (Its battlemented chimneypiece is not original, but was designed by the cabinet maker George Bullock around 1811.) [3] A single-storey great chamber (now called the Great Parlour) was built very soon afterwards on the ground floor beyond the upper end of the hall, and then in the 1550s and 1590s a sequence of family chambers was built in the west and north wings respectively. They were linked on both floors by corridors, built into the central courtyard – as at Smithills – so that it was no longer necessary to approach a second chamber through a first.

Many visitors to Speke find the courtyard, with its two tall yew-trees, damp and often dark. With hindsight, we can see that such houses were on the way to becoming old-fashioned, but a closed courtyard with a gatehouse on one side and the hall on the other was still a high-status model in the North of England, as it had been in medieval times. A recent northern example was the palatial house which Sir William Cavendish had begun at Chatsworth in 1552; another was the equally magnificent seat, begun in 1555 and finished in 1587 by Lord Burghley at Burghley House. These examples might have appealed to a conservative man like Sir Thomas Hoghton, a staunch Catholic who, rather than live in Elizabeth's increasingly Protestant England, preferred to go into exile in Flanders in 1569 (There he became a considerable benefactor of the English College, which William Allen – born at Rossall Hall – had founded at Douai in Flanders in 1568 and where many sons of Lancashire's Catholic gentry were to be educated during the next two centuries.)

2.7. Speke Hall: the open hall of *c.*1530. with its flat ceiling and the 'Romantic' chimneypiece of 1811.

Before leaving England Sir Thomas had taken down much of the medieval house on the hilltop at **Hoghton** and had begun a new courtyard house, but he did not finish it. His example was followed at **Stonyhurst** in the 1590s by Sir Richard Shireburne, who was related by marriage to the Hoghtons and was also another Catholic on the fringes of the nobility and the Court. He too began the rebuilding of his house around a courtyard at Stonyhurst, but died in 1594 before he could complete it. A similar but less ambitious, timber-framed, courtyard house is **Astley Hall** in Chorley, which was finished in the 1570s by Robert Charnock; he was another Catholic and married Isobel Norris of Speke in 1574. (There is a risk of overstating the link between Catholicism and conservative attitudes to building. Catholics, however, were a significant minority among the Lancashire gentry in the sixteenth and seventeenth centuries – and a majority in the south-west of the county. They deserve an explanatory box at the end of this chapter: see pp. 49–51.)

Taller houses

Attitudes had begun to change in the 1570s, and houses with wings built around a courtyard came to be seen as inconvenient. The idea of making space for the necessary extra rooms by increasing a building's height rather than extending its 'footprint' thereafter found favour. Height has always been an easy way of impressing people, and to build higher is easier in masonry than in timber. By the 1590s most gentry families were building new houses with a compact plan and with three storeys rather than the traditional two. Such an arrangement gave a house more impact in its setting and allowed better views from the house; it also encouraged the placing of the great chamber on the first floor – a vertical rather than a horizontal separation of rooms.

One of the earliest such houses in Lancashire is **Birchley Hall** at Billinge [2.8]. (It is now a Sue Ryder care centre and <u>not open to the public</u>, but its façade can be well seen from St Mary's Avenue). It was built in 1594 for Thurston Anderton, a member of a noted Catholic family. It has the traditional plan with a central hall and two cross-wings and has three storeys; its façade has been much remodelled, though the shapes of some former windows can still be discerned. When first built, the house did not look so tall as it does today, since the now blocked original entrance door on the *left* (which appears to be at first-floor

2.8. Birchley Hall: an almost symmetrical façade between two cross-wings, now turned around – with the original hall bay-window (now a door) on the right 'mirrored' by the original hall porch on the left.

2.9. Wythenshawe Hall: much like Birchley Hall, but with the roof of the great chamber (above the hall) rising above the cross-wings.

level) must have stood above a half-sunk service basement. This doorway was neatly integrated into the design of the façade by being placed within a full-height projecting porch, which is tucked against the left-hand cross-wing, and was matched on the *right* by another shallow projection originally containing the bay-window of the hall.

A good, timber-framed, example of such an arrangement (though heavily restored) is at **Wythenshawe Hall**, the seat of the Tatton family who were significant landowners south of Manchester [2.9]. The hall has a matching porch and bay window; the great chamber was rebuilt above the hall, apparently after a fire in the 1570s – which left the once-prominent cross-wings strangely outfaced.

Taller houses with towers

If a house still had a medieval tower in Elizabethan times – and many houses in Lancashire did – another way to gain space was to use the tower more efficiently. A good example of transforming a tower is the work said to have been done in 1596 at **Turton Tower** for William Orrell [2.10]. There are signs in the stonework that his mason stripped out the old floors and built two storeys in the space, originally used for three, and then raised the tower by some three metres of better quality, coursed, masonry, so that it could accommodate three storeys of rooms of a decent size and height. These new rooms were reception rooms – the hall on the

2.10. Turton Tower: the top floor of the tower was built around 1596 in better-quality masonry above the old tower; the tallest timber-framed building (in the centre) is the staircase tower of *c.*1650.

ground floor with the great chamber above it. Service rooms were already accommodated in a slightly earlier cruck-framed building to the north, later linked to the tower, but now largely hidden behind Victorian additions.

On the other hand, at **Borwick Hall** near Carnforth (which is <u>private</u> but visible from its gatehouse), the lower floors of the probably late-medieval tower were used for the kitchen and other service rooms [2.11]. The house shows the attempt in the 1590s by its new owner, the Kendal clothier, Robert Bindloss, to put behind him the bad old days by placing

2.11. Borwick Hall: a peaceful, well-windowed, façade, more or less symmetrical, built in front of the medieval tower in 1595.

a well-windowed and many-gabled new wing slightly in front of the tower. The new façade is roughly balanced around the full-height projection containing the porch. The hall stands to the left, with the parlour for the family's daily living in the cross-wing; the great chamber was above the hall, with the withdrawing room – into which people could withdraw from the formality or the bustle of the great chamber – over the parlour.

Buildings, in which important rooms are on upper floors, are more impressive if they have imposing staircases. In medieval times the normal form of stair was a spiral staircase, which takes up little space but has obvious disadvantages. By the mid-sixteenth century this was being superseded by the more convenient 'closed-well' staircase, in which short straight flights rise around a solid core. Borwick has the best example in Lancashire; it has a balustraded top, which bears the date 1595 and the name, not of the owner, but of the mason, Alixander Brinsmead – with whose work Bindloss must have been well pleased. (It is illustrated in plate 35 of Clare Hartwell and Nikolaus Pevsner's *North Lancashire*.) Work 'signed' by a craftsman is rare, but the large timber-framed bay windows at Little Moreton Hall, dated 1559, carry the name of the carpenter, Richard Dale, as well as that of the owner, William Moreton.

The very end of the century saw the introduction of the finer 'open-well' staircase; this was normally built of timber around the outer walls of the stairhall, which was becoming a room in its own right and – by virtue of its two-storey height – an important feature in a gentleman's house. **Turton Tower** has a somewhat later example: recent dendrochronological analysis suggests a date of around 1650 for its staircase, which was built in a specially projecting turret – to give more prominence to this major status symbol.

Building high is an easy way to impress people; building on a prominent site can often be more effective. The medieval castles at Clitheroe, Hornby and Lancaster, each built on a defensible hill, had arrogantly displayed their impregnability. The medieval predecessors of Hoghton Tower and Lathom House had also been built on an exposed site to make their mark. Similarly, a number of new Elizabethan houses seem to have been deliberately built to be seen from far and wide, as a public relations statement, and perhaps also to enjoy the view. Nationally, the best-known example is **Hardwick Hall** in Derbyshire. In Lancashire, **Gawthorpe Hall**, near Padiham, was built for the Shuttleworths, a family with rising fortunes, and was probably sited on a bluff above the river Calder, so that it would be visible from a main road and much of the estate belonging to an older gentry family, the Starkies of Huntroyde. **Haigh Hall**, near Wigan, which enjoys views over the Mersey Valley as far as Snowdonia, was rebuilt in the 1830s on the site of an Elizabethan house.

Long galleries

Among the houses mentioned so far, only Gawthorpe still has a long gallery, but there must have been one in most houses from which they have disappeared. A gallery was the Elizabethan status symbol *par excellence* – because of its obvious amenity and also, perhaps, because of the difficulty and the expense of building one. As there has always been a snobbery about being in fashion, every gentry family tried to provide one somehow. William Moreton built one into the roof space at **Little Moreton Hall** in the 1560s – a date established recently by dendrochronology – and nearly caused the south wing to collapse. The idea of galleries came from Italy via France, and they had existed in England since the reign of Henry VIII, but most were built in the twenty or so years either side of 1600. The latest gallery in the North West is probably the one at **Hutton-in-the-Forest**, near Penrith, which dates from the early 1640s.

The best position for a long room was at the top of a house. **Astley Hall** has a striking example above the hall; it was cleverly contrived, probably in the 1620s, within the front half of the original roof space. Posts take much of the weight of the roof from the mullions of the 52 windows, which form, in effect, a wall of glass. (Many of the original small, diamond-shaped panes, framed in lead strips, still exist.) The grandest long gallery in Lancashire is, however, the one at **Gawthorpe**. [2.12] It is high enough to counter the effect of its length, and has five bay windows, its original plaster ceiling and a chimneypiece, dated 1603.

Galleries were used for a variety of purposes – for entertaining guests, or for walking indoors in poor weather, while on a fine day people could just sit in the sunlit warmth of a bay window to enjoy a book, some needlework, a quiet conversation or a bird's-eye view of the garden.

2.12. Gawthorpe Hall: in the long gallery the plaster ceiling and fireplace overmantel are original and were made in 1603; the Victorian wallpaper was designed by Augustus Pugin, and the portraits date from the seventeenth century.

Galleries were often used to display portraits of family members or of people whom the owner admired. In the gallery at Towneley Hall (which stands on the top floor of the medieval tower and seems to have been converted into a corridor leading to four bedrooms in the early eighteenth century) visitors can still see the frames of family portraits, complete with titles, to remind up-and-coming generations of Towneleys of the qualities of their ancestors and thus – parents must have hoped – to stimulate an ambition to succeed in the same way. These portraits were, unfortunately, removed in 1902 and subsequently sold at auction. There are, though, good collections of family portraits at **Astley Hall, Browsholme Hall, Holker Hall, Lytham Hall, Meols Hall, Sizergh Castle** and **Tabley House.** The gallery at Gawthorpe now contains some fine seventeenth-century portraits lent to the National Trust by the National Portrait Gallery.

The most interesting portraits in a Lancashire house – they are really no more than approximate likenesses – are the remarkable sequence of fifteen in the hall at **Astley**, where, in their fashionable round-headed frames, they now form part of the panelling [2.13]. They probably date from around 1620 and may well have come from a long gallery – though not necessarily the one at Astley. Some of them – like Queen Elizabeth and Sir Francis Drake, Henry IV of France and William the Silent of Holland – are such as might have been found in many English Anglican households. It is, however, more difficult to explain the presence of Philip II of Spain, who launched the Armada, and Ambrogio Spinola, the Italian general of the Spanish army which sought to defeat the Dutch Protestants – let alone a Muslim leader like Mohammed II, who in 1453 captured Constantinople. Whoever commissioned these paintings must have been a man much more broad-minded than most of his (and our) contemporaries, a man who admired leadership more than ideology.

2.13. Astley Hall: two of the Jacobean 'portraits' in the hall panelling – Henry IV of France and Robert Dudley, Earl of Leicester.

Halls

By the middle of the sixteenth century the major drawback of the traditional full-height open hall between the two-storey cross-wings – as, for example, at Rufford – was clear: people could not pass from a private room in one wing to one in the other wing without going through the public and probably noisy space of the hall. But what could they do? The hall was still important to families as the traditional symbol of their lordship – which involved not merely leadership in, but hospitality towards, the manor community. There is no conclusive evidence, but in many cases it is reasonable to surmise that a family with a large house which, like Smithills, had been extended at the upper end, simply demoted some of the family rooms in the lower end of the house and used them as storage rooms or chambers for upper servants. (They could always be brought back into family use, if required later, for an elder son or for a poor relation.) At **Ordsall** [2.14], on the other hand, the Radclyffes moved the kitchen and other service rooms out of the lower end of the house, and then, adding a bay-window, re-used the space for finer family rooms than were possible in the old upper-end. They then built a new service-wing of brick in 1639. There were common patterns, but never a standard plan.

Despite the perceived inconvenience of the traditional hall, there was, of course, nothing to prevent an Elizabethan gentleman, who was planning a new house, from building an open hall rising through the equivalent of two storeys to the rafters of its roof. Many people at the time would have regarded this as old-fashioned, but this might not have mattered to someone of a conservative frame of mind, or someone who wanted to stress the length of his gentry pedigree and hence his importance in county society. The Masters of several Inns of Court and Oxbridge Colleges were doubtless moved by the same ideas, and similar thoughts may well have passed through the minds of Sir Thomas Hoghton at Hoghton Tower or Robert Charnock at Astley Hall. The spacious hall at **Hoghton** stands in part above a basement [2.15], and some of its details, both inside and out, suggest early-seventeenth-century

2.14. Ordsall Hall: the original hall bay to the left, and the bay of *c*.1600, added to the right of the cross-passage in front of the former service rooms.

work, so it may in fact have been finished, or 'modernised', by Sir Thomas's nephew, Sir Richard – perhaps to impress James I when he visited in 1617.

However, after the middle of the sixteenth century, many builders of new houses who were less wealthy or less pretentious, or who had simply come to feel that the inconvenience of the open-roofed hall outweighed its connotations of status, must have chosen the convenient compromise solution, offered by a fairly high single-storey hall with a low room above it. (There is a blocked doorway in a wall of the hall itself at **Little Moreton,** which suggests that William Moreton did that as early as *c.*1545 by inserting an upper floor, subsequently removed, within the body of the hall.) Such lower halls formed an imposing entrance to the house, with a detached screen to separate them from their cross-passage and service areas. All such screens in Lancashire have disappeared, though the remains of one, dated 1558, can be seen in the entrance hall at **Sizergh**.

2.15. Hoghton Tower: a photograph of *c.*1880 showing the upper courtyard with the entrance to the cross-passage of the hall up the steps and the hall bay on the right; the statue (now gone) is of William III.

One change, which had begun before the end of the Middle Ages but became general in the sixteenth century, was the separation of the entrance to the family's part of the house from the entrance to the service rooms. By Elizabethan times, most new houses had a separate entrance for servants. Wherever possible, it was placed to one side, to allow the family to pass through the house from the entrance courtyard to the garden at the back, without meeting servants and tradesmen. If the service rooms were placed in a semi-basement, as at Birchley, a side-entrance at this lower level would be a most convenient arrangement: there is a good example at **Gawthorpe**, with easy access to the stables, barn and other service buildings.

Levens Hall provides the best example of a major Elizabethan remodelling of a medieval house with its hall and tower [2.16]. Some of the details are unclear, but it is likely that, as at Sizergh, Hoghton and Birchley, the new owner in the 1590s, James Bellingham, placed his hall above a service basement (built out of the medieval hall and accessed from behind). His hall's floor was thereby almost at the level of the room above the vaulted cellar of the tower (on the visitor's left). This tower room was used to accommodate the house's great chamber – now called the Drawing Room – with a small withdrawing room beyond it. (The long gallery is thought to have been higher up, above the hall.) At the

2.16. Levens Hall, as remodelled in the 1580s: the medieval tower is hidden behind the left-hand gable, and the Elizabethan entrance was in the tower to the right.

right-hand (or lower) end of the hall the service wing was rebuilt to contain the kitchen at the rear and, at the front, was given a tall, projecting tower containing a spiral staircase for servants and the hall porch. Under the skin of new work the house thus retained its traditional plan. The hall itself is only about four metres high and has lost its screen, but it is tall enough to counter its width and has an elaborate heraldic display of the Bellingham family's pride and of its loyalty to Queen Elizabeth in the plaster frieze and ceiling. It is an impressive entrance to the house, and first impressions count.

Delight

Levens Hall also provides good examples of several of the fashionable and expensive status symbols, which most Elizabethan families felt that they owed it to themselves to display.

Large windows

Some Elizabethan status symbols were inherited from the late Middle Ages, like the bay windows in the hall and great chamber but, more generally, big windows with a grid of stone mullions and transoms to hold large expanses of expensive glass — itself a status symbol — became *de rigueur*. Most houses had them by the 1590s, and Levens is no exception. Both **Stonyhurst** and **Hoghton** had a bay-window on each side of the hall. Oriel windows, little bay-windows projecting at a higher level, were also popular, as can be seen at **Gawthorpe**.

2.17. Levens Hall: the hall with its Elizabethan panelling, ceiling and plaster frieze containing the royal arms and those of several members of the Bellingham family; the doorway in the centre leads to the original great chamber.

Plaster ceilings

The hall at **Levens** is dominated by its plaster ceiling [2.17]. In medieval times ceilings in ground-floor rooms had normally been decorated by the heavily moulded beams which carried the floor of the room above, and these can still be seen at **Smithills**, both in the parlour and in Andrew Barton's great chamber. In the middle of the sixteenth century fashion changed, and such beams were generally hidden above a flat ceiling of plaster, forced onto a base of reeds or straw. Soon these flat ceilings were decorated by thin ribs forming geometrical shapes, cast in wooden moulds and then fixed, while still damp, to the half-dry plaster of the ceiling. (There are good examples at **Sizergh**, which are, however, made of wood.) In the hall at **Levens** the plasterers went further and used such ribs to define panels in which heraldic devices – like the Bellinghams' hunting horns and stags – or other low-relief figures can be seen.

At the very end of the century ribs were superseded by wider, somewhat heavy straps, as in what is now the Drawing Room at **Gawthorpe** [2.18]. This was originally used as the 'dyninge chamber', and the acorns, oak-leaves and spiralling vine-trails between the straps are references to the god Bacchus and the pleasures of the table. Below this ceiling, which was made in 1605, is a delightful and deep plaster frieze with a running trail of stems and leaves inhabited by a variety of little birds and animals, mermaids, heraldic beasts and men and women in contemporary costume. There is another fine ceiling in the Great Parlour at **Speke**, where, perhaps in 1612, both the earlier beams and the flat panels between them were decorated with trails of vines, roses and pomegranates.

2.18. Gawthorpe Hall: mermaids and griffins in the plaster frieze of the ceiling in the former dining chamber.

2.19. Sizergh Castle: a drawing of 1888 showing the panelling in the Inlaid Room, with its intricate marquetry.

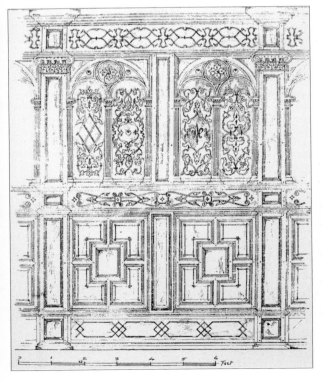

Panelling

The earliest panelling in Lancashire – at Smithills – has already been described, but the fashions for linenfold and Romayne decoration died out by about 1550. There is simple panelling of the 1590s in the hall at **Levens,** but finer work in the great chamber, which was the more important room. By then, all four sides of every panel were decorated with applied mouldings, and some large panels contained other smaller panels, square or diamond in shape. The highest-quality Elizabethan panelling has inlaid work in the panels themselves. There is good work in several houses, but the panelling in the Inlaid Room at **Sizergh** [2.19], which dates from the late 1570s, is much finer and of national importance. (Indeed, between 1891 and 1999, it was displayed at the Victoria and Albert Museum in London.) This panelling is divided into 'bays' by pilasters; the lower half of each bay has square panels within squares, but the upper half is decorated with round-headed motifs, forming a sort of arcade. In all the panels there is the most exquisite inlaid work featuring geometric designs or flowing arabesques in woods of contrasting colours.

Genuine panelling was expensive, and sometimes *trompe-l'oeil* panelling, painted onto plaster, was used as a substitute. Small examples, probably dating from the 1570s, have been uncovered in the great chamber at **Wythenshawe Hall** [2.20] and in the parlour at **Little Moreton Hall**.

Chimneypieces

The fireplace – literally as well as metaphorically the focus of a room – is almost certainly what a visitor sees first at **Levens**. It is dominated by the coat of arms of Queen Elizabeth – with the Welsh dragon as one of the supporters – carried out in painted plasterwork to create a sort of chimneypiece above it. The royal coat of arms, which stands out in a deep plaster frieze containing the shields of the members of James Bellingham's family, of his ancestors and in-laws, showed his guests that he regarded himself as a patriotic member of the powers that be and was committed to the maintenance of law and order in the area.

Finer as works of art are the several wooden chimneypieces at **Sizergh**, which date from the 1560s and are richly decorated with beautifully carved Strickland coats of arms. One in the Queen's Room displays the royal coat of arms and carries the inscription *Vivat Regina*, a clear sign of Strickland's loyalty to Elizabeth, although he was a Catholic. It bears the date 1569, the year before the pope excommunicated the queen. (For more detail on the religious history of this time see pages 49–51.)

2.20. Wythenshawe Hall: 'panelling' painted onto the plaster (and timber) wall in the great chamber, and now much faded.

2.21. Levens Hall: the chimneypiece in the former great chamber (now the drawing room) carved with the royal coat of arms above those of the Bellingham family, and with Corinthian columns correctly placed above Ionic ones.

Levens, however, has the most impressive wooden chimneypiece in our area [2.21]. Standing in the Drawing Room (once the great chamber), it is dated 1595 and contains both the royal arms and those of the Bellingham family. It is also decorated by pairs of Classical pilasters or columns, arranged in the way that the Romans had placed them on the Colosseum – with the sturdy Doric at the bottom, the graceful Ionic with its curly volutes above it, and the Corinthian, richly decorated with acanthus leaves, at the top. Bellingham's contemporaries would have seen this as a fashionable indication that he was a man of culture. Another interesting heraldic chimneypiece, dating from 1567, is in the Great Parlour at **Speke**. Its elaborate but naïve display consists, not of coats of arms, but of human figures representing three generations of the Norris family – rather like a contemporary monument in a church. More sophisticated are the fine plasterwork chimneypieces at **Gawthorpe** – one in the Huntroyde Room, which displays the Shuttleworth coat of arms with figures of Justice and Prudence as the supporters, and one in the long gallery which bears the arms of James I, supported by a lion and a unicorn. It also contains inscriptions in English and Latin to remind Shuttleworths (and others) that they should honour the king, fear God, who controlled men's destinies, do good and seek peace.

Conceits

Levens also contains a good example of what the Elizabethans called 'conceits' or 'devices'. The wooden chimneypiece in the Small Drawing Room has human figures representing the four seasons and the four elements – earth, air, fire and water – from which it was thought that everything was composed; also the five senses, the sources of the pleasures of this life, and both Samson and Hercules, a Judeo-Christian hero and a Classical one. Geoffrey Whitney, the author of *A Choice of Emblemes*, a contemporary source-book of decorative motifs published in 1586 , defined a conceit as 'some witty device with cunning [= skilful] workmanship, something obscure to be perceived at the first, whereby, when with further consideration it is understood, it may the greater delight the beholder'.[4] We need to read this definition twice before its meaning becomes clear, but it is the same with conceits: they were basically ingenious puzzles, brain-teasers, introduced to make people think, or as aids to conversation; perhaps the figures in the frieze at Gawthorpe were so intended. The most moving Elizabethan conceits in the North West are the plaster bas-reliefs at either end of the long gallery at **Little Moreton Hall**, which play on the perils of ignorance and the power given by knowledge [2.22]. It takes but little imagination to see William Moreton, some four centuries ago, anxiously encouraging his sons to work hard at school, lest they become the pawns of fate.

Classical motifs

The figure of Hercules in the Small Drawing Room at Levens is a reminder that Elizabeth's reign was the period in which all educated men and women became aware of the Roman world. Some were, moreover, fascinated by Roman ideas about life and art, since these challenged those of Christianity and revealed a sort of New World, a mental equivalent of the Americas. The earliest use of a Classical motif in Lancashire probably dates from the 1560s and is at **Hoghton Tower**. Above the gateway leading to the lower courtyard [2.23], a pair of tiny Ionic columns frame a small decorative plaque which shows the initials TH (for Thomas Hoghton) and a man wrestling with a lion. This was often thought to represent the Old Testament hero, Samson, who was regarded by the medieval Church as a symbol of the successful struggle of good over evil,

2.22. Little Moreton Hall: plaster conceits in the long gallery, showing (on the left) the wheel of fortune whose rule is ignorance, and (on the right) the sphere of destiny whose ruler is knowledge. The Latin inscription on the wheel means 'whoever climbs up like this will fall down at once'.

2.23. Hoghton Tower: perhaps the earliest Classical motifs in Lancashire: two Ionic colonnettes framing a struggle between a man and a beast – dating from the 1560s.

but it is – I believe – more likely to portray Hercules strangling the lion of Nemea, a Classical story with the same theme.

Incomparably more grandiose is the front of the tall gatehouse at **Stonyhurst**, begun in 1592, which is an affirmation of Sir Richard Shireburne's power, his pride in his ancient lineage and his contemporary culture [2.1]. The triumphal arch, which gives form to the lowest stage, was a Roman motif, and the four tiers of paired Classical columns are correctly placed one above the other – with the Composite (the most ornate, combining Corinthian acanthus leaves with Ionic volutes) at the top. Shireburne was a senior officer in the household of the Earl of Derby and may well have seen the fine three-storey tower, dated 1585, in the courtyard of Burghley House, where Queen Elizabeth's chief minister lived. (Like a number of Elizabethan nobles, Lord Burghley was well acquainted with contemporary French architecture – which was a source of many new ideas at the time – and his tower was probably derived from a similar gateway designed around 1550 for the château of Anet – now visible outside the Ecole des Beaux-Arts in Paris.) The gatehouse at Stonyhurst may have been the source for the chimneypiece at Levens; it was certainly emulated around and above the front door [2.24] at **Browsholme**, when Thomas Parker came to rebuild his house soon after he had purchased the freehold of the estate from the Crown in 1603.

There is a fine three-storey gatehouse near **Horwich**, which was built in 1591 to guard the long-demolished timber-framed **Lostock Hall**. (It is private but visible from Ox Hey Lane.) Its (now blocked) gateway and the broad windows above it are flanked by pairs of correctly placed Classical columns. A plainer but still fine, two-storey gatehouse, dated 1561, stands at **Martholme** near Great Harwood, and a very late example, dated 1650, can be seen at **Borwick**.

Educated Elizabethans were well read in the Latin classics and many of them looked back more than a thousand years and sought in their present to recreate something of the recently discovered values and beauties of the Roman world. The decorative details of the Classical orders at Stonyhurst and Browsholme are fairly accurate, but the columns were used without any appreciation of the fact that in Roman times they were not just decorative motifs, but were part of a series of conventions, based on modular proportions, which laid down, among other things, that upper columns should be taller than lower ones – which is not the case at Stonyhurst. Although most of Sir Richard's contemporaries knew more about Roman architecture than their fathers had done, they still regarded it as no more than a fashionable storehouse from which they could take and use any decorative details which caught their fancy. Mark Girouard put it beautifully when he wrote that 'the Elizabethans approached the classical treasury in the spirit of pirates, rather than disciples'.[5]

2.24. Browsholme Hall: the entrance (of *c.*1605) which must have been influenced by the gatehouse at Stonyhurst.

Symmetrical façades

During the long reign of Elizabeth yet another Roman idea was introduced to England via France, the idea that the façade of a gentleman's house should be symmetrical – to reflect the symmetry of the human body and symbolise the order of the universe. The façades of later-medieval houses had been designed in a balanced way, with a pair of gables flanking the hall to fit the traditional plan of hall and cross-wings, but the front door had always led into the *lower* end – not the centre – of the hall. External symmetry was difficult to achieve in front of these traditional houses. Most educated people appreciated it, but few made strenuous efforts to build symmetrical façades in front of the still convenient traditional plans.

A number of gentlemen were, however, prepared to make small steps towards symmetry. A second bay window was added in the 1590s, in front of an unimportant room at **Speke**, so that the façade of the wing in the courtyard, facing the entrance, should appear symmetrical without too much expense. Much the same was done a little later on the entrance front at **Ordsall** (see p. 37).

A more innovative approach was to design the façade so that the projection to house the hall porch was balanced by the projecting bay-window at the upper end of the hall. As mentioned before, this had been done as early as the 1570s at **Wythenshawe Hall** and was repeated at **Birchley** in 1594, but the best example is at **Hacking Hall** (a private house, but visible from a footpath), which was built in 1607 for the judge, Sir Thomas Walmesley [2.25]. Its plan has been published;[6] it shows that the entrance on the right leads into the lower end of the hall, giving a good view of a substantial fireplace; that the main stair is at the back of the upper, left-hand, wing; and that the great chamber was above the hall, again with a fine fireplace. (The attic storey was open from end to end and may perhaps have served as a long gallery.) Such a plan was convenient and also had the advantage of making the front of the house appear more or less symmetrical; it and the plentiful gables also gave a nice play of projection and recession to the façade. (The upper-end chamber on the left on the first floor had a privy corbelled out from the wall, as in a medieval house like the so-called Stokesay Castle; most owners, however, preferred to use a close stool in the chamber itself.)

Only a few men adopted the more radical approach, where the façade is symmetrical around a central entrance, with the plan fitted in behind as well as possible. Perhaps the earliest example in Lancashire is **Hough End Hall** in Chorlton-cum-Hardy, Manchester [2.26]. (The house is now

2.25. Hacking Hall: a nearly symmetrical façade with the porch on the right matched by the hall bay on the left.

2.26. Hough End Hall: a photograph of *c*.1980, showing the almost symmetrical façade in which the hall window (to the right of the door) is only slightly bigger than the pantry window on the left.

<u>private</u> offices, but is visible from Nell Lane). It was new-built of bricks on a stone plinth in 1596 for Nicholas Mosley, after he had bought the manor of Manchester. He came from a Manchester merchant family and had made a fortune in London, where he was soon to be elected the Lord Mayor, and knighted. He was clearly a man who was aware of the latest fashions: he died in 1612, and his fine monument in Didsbury church is the earliest in Lancashire to use Classical columns. Both the main floors of his house – whose windows are tall with transoms as well as mullions – are now open-plan offices, but the original plan has been published.[6] This shows an almost central entrance which led to the lower end of the hall. The hall window on the right of the porch is matched on the left by the (slightly smaller) window of the pantry, behind which was a corridor leading to the staircase. These rooms were framed by the withdrawing room in the right wing, and by the kitchen and the family's adjacent winter parlour in the left wing. A contemporary Lancastrian might have called it a waste of space and money to give his pantry almost as big a window as his hall, but Mosley probably regarded this feature proudly as the height of contemporary aristocratic fashion and thus a symbol of his importance. The building of gentry houses – in Elizabethan and later times – was not just a matter of acquiring improved accommodation, but also of displaying enhanced status in a competitive society.

The finest example in Lancashire of a symmetrical façade with a central porch taking precedence over the house's plan is at **Gawthorpe Hall**. It was designed in the 1590s and built for the Shuttleworth family, but was not finished until 1607; I shall describe it in the next chapter. It is still a compromise solution: a symmetrical façade could not be fully integrated with a symmetrical plan until the status of the hall declined, but this did not happen before the mid-seventeenth century.

Roman Catholics and gentry house building

After the Reformation, more than a third of Lancashire's gentry retained their allegiance to the Old Faith of Roman Catholicism. This was in part due to the fact that in the 1500s Lancashire – except the Manchester-Bolton area, whose trade in textiles opened it to the outside world – was a peripheral place, something of a backwoods region, more or less self-sufficient and therefore somewhat conservative and suspicious towards new ideas. Lancaster is, for example, 230 miles from London, as compared with York (190 miles) and Chester (180 miles). Lancashire was, furthermore, an area on the way to nowhere. If a man needed to go from London to Scotland, he took the Great North Road to Edinburgh through York, and if he had to go to Ireland, he went to Dublin via Chester.

Moreover, the clergy of the (Roman Catholic) Church in the reign of Henry VIII seem to have enjoyed the respect of most Lancastrians, and many people were doubtless reluctant to change their familiar and time-honoured ways of worship at the dictate of a distant London. The newly created diocese of Chester, which included Lancashire, was large but poorly funded; perhaps for these reasons the bishops tended to lack fervour. Their life was not made easier by the fact that the fourth Earl of Derby, who was the Lord Lieutenant of Lancashire for most of Elizabeth's reign and thus responsible for raising the militia in times of war and for maintaining law and order in peacetime, had Catholic relatives and was reluctant to use much force to impose religious uniformity. If he had done so, Lancashire might have become as Anglican as the rest of England, but he did not, and it did not.

To be a practising Catholic – to be a 'recusant' or person who refused to take Holy Communion according to the Anglican form of worship – was technically a crime from 1559 until the Catholic Relief Act of 1791. Elizabeth's England was no different from most countries on the Continent, where religious practice was a matter of state, and the convention was that subjects followed the religion of their ruler. To refuse to do so made one politically suspect – someone who might, by undermining the unity of the national church, undermine the social order as well. The queen was more concerned with public conformity than with private faith and was prepared at first to tolerate gentlemen who only attended church occasionally; but the situation changed for the worse in 1570 when Pope Pius V excommunicated her as a heretic, thereby in theory releasing her Catholic subjects from their allegiance and lending tacit support to rebellion in favour of Mary, Queen of Scots. This placed most Catholics in an impossible dilemma: should they as Englishmen support the queen, or as Catholics heed the pope's implied injunction? The government felt obliged to believe that every Catholic was a potential traitor, and there were enough hotheads to give credence to their fears, and to smear all Lancastrians in the eyes of outsiders. (In my own lifetime we have seen several periods marked by an atmosphere of suspicion and fear – notably during the Cold War.) Many gentlemen declared their loyalty to the queen by displaying the royal arms prominently in their houses; there are good examples both at Sizergh Castle, the home of the Catholic Stricklands, and at nearby Levens Hall, the seat of the Anglican Bellinghams.

After 1570 heavy fines and prison sentences were imposed on Catholic gentlemen to encourage them (and their tenants) to conform at least outwardly. Sir Richard Shireburne's son was more devout than his father and was therefore more heavily fined, with the result that he could not finish the rebuilding of Stonyhurst. A more visible reminder of the sufferings of Elizabethan Catholics who would not take the easy way out by an occasional appearance at the services of the Church of England is a portrait at Towneley Hall, painted in about 1600. This shows John and Mary Towneley and their fourteen children, and also records the substantial fines – more than £5000, or at least a million pounds in our money – and the long periods in prison in various parts of the country, which Towneley had had to endure for maintaining a Catholic place of worship in the area.

Nevertheless, many Catholics preferred to follow the faith of their fathers, even though this meant that they were excluded from a university education in England and a career in politics or the public service above the level of the parish. Fortunately for them, many Anglican gentlemen in Lancashire liked their Catholic neighbours well enough to turn a blind eye to their recusancy.

Conditions were easier during the reigns of James I and Charles I, but most Catholics chose what became the losing side in major political controversies – which, of course, strengthened the perception among governments and their supporters that Catholics were threats to society. At the time of the Civil War a third of Lancashire gentlemen were Catholics, and therefore more actively sympathetic to the king, who had a Catholic wife, than to a Parliament which they believed to be anti-Catholic. In 1715 a number of Lancashire Catholic gentlemen supported the 'Jacobite' rebellion led by James Stuart, the 'Old Pretender', and afterwards a few lost their lives and many others their lands. These severe government reprisals made most people think twice before joining Bonnie Prince Charlie in 1745, and during the rest of the century many Catholics decided to conform. By 1801 Catholics amounted to only 1%

of the population of England – but a quarter of them lived in Lancashire. Despite all of this, several of the finest houses in the county – like Croxteth, Towneley, Lytham and Scarisbrick, not to mention smaller ones like Sizergh and Leighton – were built or extended by Catholic families, when they felt it safe to do so. Perhaps they were able to do this because they could not spend their money on the expenses of political life and public office.

References

1   Quoted in G.E. Mingay, *The Gentry* (1976), p. 5.

2   Thomas Macaulay, *History of England*, quoted in G.E. Mingay, *The Gentry* (1976), p. xi.

3   Clive Wainwright, Introduction to *George Bullock, Cabinet Maker*, published for H. Blairman and Sons by John Murray (1988).

4   Quoted in Mark Girouard, *Robert Smythson and the Elizabethan Country House* (1983), p. 27.

5   Mark Girouard, Robert Smythson and the Elizabethan Country House (1983), p. 18.

6   Clare Hartwell and Nikolaus Pevsner, *Lancashire: North* (2009), p. 108, shows the ground floor, while Nicholas Cooper, *Houses of the Gentry, 1480–1680* (1999), p. 2, presents two floors.

7   Clare Hartwell and Nikolaus Pevsner, *Lancashire: Manchester and the South East* (2004), p. 415.

3.1. Astley Hall: a painting of *c.*1700 showing the south wing's underlying brickwork structure, its highly glazed and almost symmetrical façade, and (in the background) a small vernacular gentry house.

CHAPTER THREE

Gentry Houses in the Seventeenth Century

Introduction

The seventeenth century is one of the most interesting in English (and European) history; it was in many areas – politics, science, religion – an important age of transitions. In the area of gentry house-building as well it witnessed the slow process by which 'vernacular' houses, with their hall and cross-wings, designed and built by one and the same man working in a local, slowly evolving and craft-based tradition, were superseded around 1700 by houses which were normally three-storeyed and symmetrical; they were, furthermore, were designed by a man, who called himself an architect and regarded himself as a gentleman, imbued with a London-based culture and following national fashions, and having little wish to have any link with the actual building process.

There was, however, no seamless web of evolution, quite simply because of the Civil War (between Charles I and his parliament) and its effects. Before hostilities broke out in 1642, most people must have assumed that life would go on much as it had in the reigns of James I and, even, Elizabeth. However, the Civil War brought gentry-house-building to a virtual standstill everywhere for ten years, and its special after-effects in Lancashire, where the authority of nearly half of the gentry families had been challenged, meant that few had the money and the confidence to build houses for at least another generation. These were indeed locust years.

An unbroken story of gentry house-building in England *can* be told, using houses built within fifty miles or so of London, but in Lancashire there are two important gaps – the years before the Civil War, and those after the Restoration of Charles II in 1660. It was tempting to leave out this chapter and to 'attach' houses built before the Civil War to the Elizabethan age and those built after it to the Georgian period. Such a division would have been neater, but would not have corresponded to the reality of how things were. House-building by the gentry petered out in Lancashire by 1640 and hardly started again before 1690. This may be sad, but is also significant, since it points up the contrast: in 1640 the design of gentry houses in Lancashire was still basically traditional and local, but by 1690 it was influenced by fashions from London.

Builders

Almost all the gentry houses in Lancashire, built both before the Civil War and afterwards, were owned by members of well established families. There were a very few exceptions – houses built with money made through the law, like Gawthorpe Hall or Clegg Hall, or through trade, like **Carr House,** near Bretherton – a <u>private</u> house, but just visible from the B5248. [3.2] The lintel of its porch carries a long inscription which relates that the house was built in 1613 for John Stones by his brothers Thomas, a London haberdasher, and Andrew, a merchant in Amsterdam, 'of their own charges'.

It is reasonable to surmise that John was the eldest son, who continued to work the family's land in Hoole, while his younger brothers sought and made fortunes in trade and then ploughed some of them back into their brother's house, and the local church, for the sake of their family's local standing. In 1628 Thomas Stones was one of those who endowed what is now St Michael's church in Much Hoole as a chapel of ease within Croston parish. In 1633 John Stones gave the font in the church.

The house itself is also one of the most interesting of the period. It was built of brick – a fairly early use in Lancashire – and has a symmetrical plan – again, another early example; its three-storey façade is also symmetrical, with a central, gabled porch and two slightly projecting cross-wings, which also had gables originally.

3.2. Carr House, Bretherton: a photograph of *c.*1980, showing the symmetry of the façade, and the diamond patterns in the brickwork.

Commodity (and delight) before the Civil War

Gawthorpe Hall was an appropriate place to end the last chapter, since it is the finest example in Lancashire of 'Elizabethan' design; when finished in 1607, it was the most up-to-date house in the county – a new building, indeed, but also a dead end [3.3]. With its symmetrical façade dominated by windows with both transoms and mullions, it was undoubtedly a striking house to look at. It was compact in form and three storeys tall above a basement, from which a spiral staircase took servants to all floors; it had prominent full-height bay-windows, which increased the vertical emphasis of the façade and also gave an interest to the shape of the rooms which they lit; its roofline had a plain parapet, which was considered more sophisticated than the gables at Hough End Hall; and the stairtower, from which the flat roof was accessible, was surrounded by the house's chimneys, which gave a further vertical emphasis. Its young owner, Richard Shuttleworth, who had inherited it from his uncle in 1608, must have been very proud, as he walked his even younger bride up to the front door later that year. We cannot know what her reaction was, on entering, but it must have been one of bewilderment, because the house's plan was unconventional to the point of being bizarre. Without her husband to guide her, she cannot have known which way to turn.

As visitors to any house, we tend to think first in terms of what Sir Henry Wotton (see p.2) called Delight, but to almost all of the people who built these houses Commodity was more important and meant

3.3. Gawthorpe Hall: a lithograph of *c*.1840, showing the house before its remodelling in 1850–52; the façade is dominated by its windows, and the chimneys are placed centrally.

above all a convenient plan. Sir Francis Bacon put it succinctly in the very first sentence of his *Essay on Building*, published in 1625, when he wrote: 'Houses are built to live in, not look on; therefore let use be preferred to uniformity [= symmetry], except where both may be had.'[1] In the next sentence he went on in worldly-wise mode to say: 'Leave the goodly fabric of houses for beauty only to the enchanted palaces of the poets, who build them with small cost.' Early seventeenth-century decorative details were much the same as those in the late sixteenth century, so there is no separate section on Delight in this half of this chapter.

The plan of Gawthorpe [3.4] was a novel and ingenious experiment, an attempt to solve the Elizabethan house-designer's major problem of reconciling a central door in a symmetrical façade with a more or less traditional layout. As the figure shows, the solution was sought firstly by making the centre of the house two rooms deep, giving it what we (and people then) call a 'double-pile' plan, and secondly by turning the traditional plan through a right angle. This meant that the hall occupied the right-hand, back quarter of the house and was reached not by a *cross-passage* from the front door, but by a passage in the middle of the house running *parallel* to the façade, with service rooms opening off it towards the front of the house and the hall at the back. This passage was reached

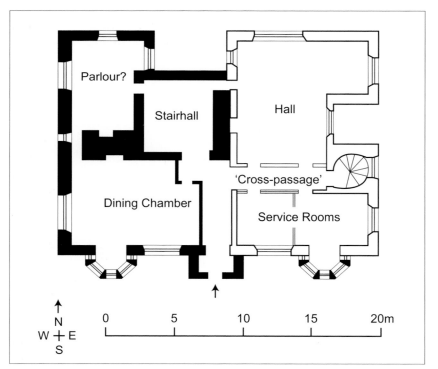

3.4. Gawthorpe Hall: the original plan: the right-hand half (in outline) shows how the traditional medieval plan was turned through a right angle and then extended; the thick walls in the centre are not the remains of a medieval tower but contained the house's chimney flues.

from the front door down a corridor leading to the stairhall at the back of the house; this route must have been dark, with no view of the welcoming hall fireplace – hardly an appropriate entrance to a gentleman's house. There was, furthermore, no easy access from the hall to the great chamber (originally known as the Dining Chamber and now as the Drawing Room) which was on the left at the front of the house.

The floor plans and façades of Gawthorpe were probably designed by Robert Smythson (*c.* 1535–1614), the first 'national name' to appear on the Lancashire stage. He had designed **Wollaton Hall**, near Nottingham, in 1580 and **Hardwick Hall** (which has a double-pile plan) in 1590 for the Dowager Countess of Shrewsbury ('Bess of Hardwick'). He had a very fertile mind which produced many ingenious designs. At Hardwick (which is much bigger than Gawthorpe) he had solved the designer's problem by turning the hall through ninety degrees, so that it was entered in the centre of one of its shorter sides. Not all his plans were practical, though. I surmise that he may even have seen the inconveniences of the plan used at Gawthorpe, and have thrown it away – only to find that someone had picked it up for Shuttleworth to build. However that may be, Smythson had no hand in the actual construction of these houses; he merely provided the plan, which was built by craftsmen. Gawthorpe was therefore very probably the first house in Lancashire to be built outside the vernacular tradition. Most of the early-seventeenth-century estate accounts for Gawthorpe still exist and they include many entries which relate to the building of the house between 1600 and 1607.[2] They allow us not merely to see how this house was built, but also give insights into traditional house-building generally – see the Appendix on Firmness.

'Traditional' house-plans

Shuttleworth must have hoped that his new house would be the model which every gentleman would copy, but this hope was only satisfied in part. Gawthorpe's symmetrical façade was more or less copied at Haigh Hall, where Anthony Whytehead, the master mason at Gawthorpe, went when he had finished his work there; and the façade of Haigh Hall was probably the model for Astley Hall and, perhaps, of Hall o' th' Hill (the private home of the Chorley Golf Club). The Jacobean Haigh Hall is no longer standing, since it was demolished and replaced by the present house in the 1830s. Its plan is unknown, but its appearance is known from the background of the portrait, painted around 1750, of its then owner, Sir Roger Bradshaigh, and his wife.[3]

However, Gawthorpe's plan was too inconvenient to provide a good model to copy; instead, almost every house built before the Civil War continued to use the traditional plan – the plan of a house in which everyone felt at home – where the entrance to the house was off-centre and led to the lower end of the hall, with the service wing on the other side of the cross passage.

The most accessible of these 'conservative' houses is **Heskin Hall**, which is now an antiques showroom near Wrightington [3.5]. It was built in brick for a member of the Mawdesley family and was described as 'new hall' in 1666, though it looks to be a generation older. It still has a single-pile plan with a hall and two gabled cross-wings, all with two-storey bay windows with mullions and transoms. The porch, which gives access to the lower end of the hall, with an immediate view of the fireplace, is placed next to the right-hand cross-wing. The great chamber was beyond the hall, in the left-hand gabled wing; its fine panelling is divided by Ionic pilasters. The original staircase was probably behind the lower end of the hall – where the main staircase is now – and perhaps in a stair tower. It gave access not merely to the chamber floor, but also to a long gallery in the attic. The kitchen was in the large rear wing on the right, which also has two upper storeys of lodgings, approached up a spiral staircase with a privy on each floor – an arrangement rather like the one at Sizergh, though at the back of the house

The most interesting house of this period in Lancashire is, however, **Astley Hall** [3.6]. It was new-built in the 1570s, when the Charnock family had to move to Chorley, and was originally entered from the north – at the back of the present house. Its subsequent history is controversial, but my view is that the original, two-storey, timber-framed courtyard house with a full-height hall was remodelled in an 'innovative' way around 1620 – perhaps to mark the accession in 1616 of Thomas

3.5. Heskin Hall: the façade is fairly symmetrical, with the porch tucked against the right-hand cross-wing.

3.6. Astley Hall (Chorley): an almost symmetrical façade, with tall bays placed on either side of the entrance and in front of the earlier timber-framed structure; the unbroken row of windows on the top floor light the long gallery.

Charnock, who had married Bridget Molyneux, a member of the wealthy Catholic family in South Lancashire. This work involved re-fronting the hall on the south of the courtyard with a brick-built, three-storey entrance façade and adding a long gallery in part of the roof-space above the hall. (The façade was rendered in about 1790, but its original appearance can be seen in a painting of around 1700 [3.1] in the Dining Room – which also shows in the background a traditional gentry house with a hall and cross-wings.)

The new façade is fairly symmetrical, with a full-height, five-sided bay window with mullions and transoms on either side of the porch, which has paired, approximately Ionic, columns. Placing the entrance door so that it gave access directly into the hall, rather than – as originally – across a courtyard, 'modernised' the house, by making it appear to visitors to have a tall, compact plan. The doorway leads into the lower end of the tall and spacious hall almost opposite the fireplace, now decorated by a tall wooden chimneypiece with three tiers of rather skinny Classical columns – probably a nineteenth-century confection. The original staircase appears to have been built at the upper end of the hall – to the right as visitors enter.

An intriguing house of this period is **Clegg Hall** near Milnrow [3.7], which was probably built around 1620 by a lawyer from a gentry family, called Theophilus Assheton. It has long been a roofless shell and dangerous to enter, but its plan is printed.[4] This and its façade show something of the way in which houses were evolving at this time. The plan was half-conservative in that the front door still led to the lower end of the hall, but half-innovative in that it was of the 'double-pile' form with a middle wall between the front and back (within which all the

3.7. Clegg Hall: a photograph of *c.*1880 showing an almost symmetrical façade with its porch decorated with roughly Classical columns.

chimney flues rise); the staircase stood between the two back rooms; and, furthermore, the kitchen and service rooms were in the basement, as at Gawthorpe, and were entered from the back of the house. Similarly, the façade was half-traditional in that its tall mullioned and transomed windows were crowned by three gables, but it was also half-innovative since it was symmetrical and had a two-storey porch framed between more or less classical columns (which have now disappeared).

Significant work before the Civil War was also carried out at **Towneley Hall** in the 1620s [3.8]. The family had survived the severe financial penalties attached to their stubborn loyalty to their Catholic faith and now felt able to embark on additions which would show the Shuttleworths at Gawthorpe (who had by then outfaced the Starkies of Huntroyde) which family really was the leading one in the area. The work involved a new hall, built above cellars in the west wing, and a new family wing (on the north, or the visitor's right), which rises through three storeys and roughly matches the medieval tower on the left, creating thereby a balanced design for the entrance courtyard. This north wing contained the kitchen in the north-west corner, and other service rooms on the ground floor, with family rooms above. The family dining chamber bears the date 1628. The upper floors in both the new wing and the medieval tower were (and are) reached by staircases (subsequently re-built) in two new square towers, which rise in the angles of the courtyard above the level of the adjacent roofs.

This Jacobean hall (which was replaced in the 1720s by the present two-storey hall – see pp. 97–99) appears from a plan of around 1700 to have had a balcony at the south end;[5] from this I surmise that the body

3.8. Towneley Hall: the (slightly altered) symmetrical Jacobean façade, with its two staircase towers in the corners between the medieval tower on the left and the *c.*1625 wing on the right. The porch was added *c.*1815.

of the hall was open to the roof. A high hall, as one can see from the roughly contemporary work at Hoghton, is always impressive, and its existence would moreover explain the provision of two stair towers to give separate access to the two wings. More intriguingly, the plan also shows that the hall had a central entrance; this was probably a late-seventeenth-century 'modernisation', but if it was an original part of the Jacobean design, it and the pair of stair towers would have created a symmetrical façade *and* plan – an early example of this feature.

'Double-pile' house plans

Of all the houses described so far, only Gawthorpe and Clegg Hall have a double-pile plan, but the advantages of such houses were well appreciated, at least in Court circles. Sir Francis Bacon, towards the end of his *Essay on Building*, wrote about a U-shaped house, perhaps like the palatial house of his near-neighbour, the Earl of Salisbury, at Hatfield: 'Let all three sides be a double house, without through lights on the sides, [so] that you may have rooms [away] from the sun, both for forenoon and afternoon'.[6] In the 1660s the gentleman architect, Sir Roger Pratt, praised the double pile for another reason, by writing that 'we have there much room in a little compass'.[7] He meant that a plan two rooms deep, which doubled the area of the centre of the house, made it easier to lay out rooms conveniently around a central hall – often with corridors to improve circulation.

Pratt had the benefit of hindsight and could see the convenience of the new plan; but to people in the early years of the century the double pile presented not merely the intellectual problem of novelty, but also the practical problems of lighting rooms which can only have windows in one wall, and of roofing a building which might be twice as deep as traditional ones – not to mention the problem of trying to make the façade more or less symmetrical, as fashion was dictating. We know, with hindsight, that the answers lie in larger windows and new types of roof trusses (see the Appendix on Firmness, p. 174) but these answers had to be discovered by trial, and error.

If the Civil War had not broken out, a double-pile house like Clegg Hall would almost certainly have been copied and modified elsewhere in Lancashire during the 1630s and 1640s. Maybe it was, but there is now no evidence of this. In the Home Counties, however, where members of the Court and wealthy City merchants vied for prestige, architects developed houses which combined a symmetrical façade and a symmetrical plan. By adopting the double-pile plan and by placing an entrance at one side or in a basement for people coming to the house to work, they managed to lead visitors, whom owners wished to impress, through a central door into the centre of a rectangular hall. One of the first houses nationally to achieve this was West Woodhay House in Berkshire. With its slightly projecting cross-wings under hipped roofs, it looks like a house built in 1686, but it was in fact built in 1636 for Sir Benjamin Rudyard, a lawyer and MP who knew several leading architects. [8] There was no time for its design to 'trickle down' to Lancashire before 1642, but it was widely copied in the Home Counties in the 1670s and '80s and can be seen in Lancashire at Wrightington Hall [5.3]; this house was not, however, built until around 1720.

The central door to the centre of the hall of such a house was only achieved by demoting the hall from its traditional, symbolic status as a semi-communal room – by making it no longer the imposing first room in a manor house, with a lower and an upper end, but only the first imposing room in the lord of the manor's private house. Langland had bewailed in 1380 the fact that the lord was leaving the hall for his servants to eat in;[9] by 1680, while the upper servants in older houses continued to eat in the hall, most servants in newly-built houses lived and ate in a servants' hall in a semi-basement, and were only to be seen in the main hall when required on service. A significant step had been taken by the middle of the century: as more careers were opened to gentlemen – in the law, the army and the navy, for example – fewer younger sons stayed at home to serve in their elder brother's household, and their places as upper servants were taken by men who were not born gentlemen; within what had always been a hierarchical framework, relations with servants therefore became more formal, and a gentleman's household was no longer his 'family'. This step was not taken in Lancashire until the very end of the seventeenth century, when grandsons found themselves able to act as their grandfathers had been unwilling to do.

The Civil War and its consequences

The Civil War divided friends and neighbours and even some families: Sir Gilbert Hoghton fought for the King, but his son Richard supported Parliament. The war marked a real break in the political life of England and created a significant pause in the nation's cultural life. Parliament's victory, however, served the interests of the gentry as a whole, in that the feudal system was finally abolished; it had been breaking down for generations, as money increasingly replaced service as the rent for a property. After the war land was no longer held, even indirectly, from the king, and any man with a good title to a parcel of land was regarded as its legal owner. And if he owned enough land, so that the rents from his tenant farmers meant that he had no need to work to make a living, he could call himself a gentleman.

Nationally, more than 150 important houses were destroyed during the Civil War, and Lancashire lost its fair share. The Derbys' stronghold at Lathom House and the Girlington family's Thurland Castle were badly damaged during sieges and then slighted. Several other houses were damaged to a lesser degree, notably Hoghton Tower where the medieval tower blew up after a short siege in 1642.

For gentry families two unforeseen, but unsurprising, results of the war were that more died out in the male line than would have seemed probable in 1642, and that many were impoverished for a long time, even if they were on the ultimately victorious Royalist side. Estates which had been *confiscated* by Parliament from Royalist supporters were almost always returned to their previous owners after the Restoration. However, lands which owners had had to *sell* to pay fines for 'treason' – and such fines were doubled for Catholic families – or debts, stayed in the hands of their new owners. Furthermore, debts outlived the war and the Commonwealth and still needed to be paid off after the Restoration. Such a process often took many years and must have contributed to the decline of some families and to the consolidation of some estates in the hands of more fortunate, or more cautious, ones. Only after the debts had been repaid could the head of a family think of building anything significant. The situation was exacerbated in the next generation when – thanks to William III's war with France – land taxes were high; families with little ready cash had to mortgage or sell land to meet their obligations.

Commodity in gentry houses built after the Civil War

A little building work was nevertheless carried out for Lancashire gentry clients during the Commonwealth and the early years of the Restoration, but in all cases the houses were traditional in plan and appearance. A good example is the two-storey, stone-built west wing of **Hall i' th' Wood**, near Bolton, which was added to the timber-framed house in 1648 by Alexander Norris. He was the son of a Bolton clothier, who had bought the house and estate in 1635, and, though related to the Catholic Norrises at Speke, was an ambitious Parliamentarian and responsible for the disposal of the estates which had been confiscated from Royalist gentry in Lancashire. (His daughter Margaret was to take this house and a fine dowry to John Starkie of Huntroyde.) His new wing [3.9] roughly balances the gable of the older house and provides a central entrance porch with a round-headed doorway. Otherwise it is traditional: the wide windows have mullions and transoms, and there is a canted bay window on both floors. Just inside the porch rises an attractive open-well staircase with turned balusters and newel posts.

Another such house was the tall and many-gabled **Astley Hall**, now a community centre at Astley near Leigh [3.10]. It was built in 1650 by Adam Mort, whose family had owned the estate for some fifty years. From its appearance, it could have been built around 1600. The entrance porch is more or less central, but leads to the low end of the hall, and the façade is not symmetrical. Oxendale Hall, near Osbaldeston (a <u>private</u> house, but visible from a footpath) was also built for a minor gentleman, Lawrence Osbaldeston, in 1656, but its appearance [3.11] with two storeys,

3.9. Hall i' th' Wood the wing of 1648 with its round-headed doorway but otherwise traditional windows and details.

3.10. Astley Hall (near Leigh): a balanced rather than symmetrical façade of 1650, with traditional details.

3.11. Oxendale Hall: a traditional design of 1656, with no attempt at symmetry.

a single cross-wing and a projecting porch and two gabled dormer windows fronting the attic is that of a house which might have been built at almost any time in the previous hundred years. A third house is New Hall, Clayton-le-Dale (also <u>private</u> but visible from the B6245) which was built in 1665 by George Talbot, a member of a family of middling importance. It has three storeys, and its three-gabled façade is symmetrical, but its centrally-placed porch leads into a dark vestibule rather than to a welcoming hall.

All these houses were modelled on older houses; so, but only to an extent, was the brick-built service wing (dated 1662) which was added by the Midlands-based guardian of the young Thomas Hesketh at **Rufford Old Hall** [3.12]. Out of its context it might pass for a traditional farmhouse, but its windows are no longer of the broad mullioned and transomed type. Instead each is narrow in form under a segmental relieving arch, with a single mullion and transom forming a cross – which encouraged taller rooms inside and gives a greater vertical emphasis to the façade. Such 'cross-windows', in which one of the lower lights contained a side-hung casement, had recently become fashionable in the Home Counties. The door, which led into the kitchen, was originally placed off-centre, one bay to the right.

Delight in gentry houses built after the Restoration

Some building work for gentlemen clients did take place after the Restoration, but, with the exception of the work at **Astley Hall** (in Chorley: *not* the identically-named building near Leigh shown in 3.10), it did not amount to much – less for the general reasons relating to money, already mentioned, than because of factors which were more specific to Lancashire. Firstly, the eighth and ninth Earls of Derby, the only important noblemen resident in Lancashire, did their duty as the king's

3.12. Rufford Old Hall: the 1662 service wing (now more symmetrical than originally) with the newly fashionable cross-windows.

Lord Lieutenant, but were not ambitious to play a role in national politics and were seldom at Court. (Very briefly, they resented the way in which Charles II had not, as they saw it, repaid the sacrifice of the seventh earl, who had served Charles I. He had been captured and executed in 1651, with the result that the Derby family's landholdings had been diminished both by confiscations by the republican government and by sales – and not restored after 1660.) An important link to London was thereby broken.

Secondly, the relatively high proportion of families who remained faithful to their traditional Catholicism meant that fewer young men from Lancashire studied at the Inns of Court and the universities – because Catholics were excluded. They therefore had less chance to meet other gentlemen who might be interested in architecture – or to marry young women from outside the county. The result was that fewer Lancashire gentlemen had an idea of the fashionable models to follow. (In a hierarchical society, innovations can only be introduced by leaders in that society.) Works at several major houses, built in neighbouring counties north and south in the 1670s and '80s – such as Eaton Hall (since demolished) and Lyme Park in Cheshire, and Hutton-in-the-Forest and Appleby Castle in Cumbria – were more up-to-date in London terms than at Lancashire houses. Much of Yorkshire, however, (apart from the vicinity of York) was equally conservative.

The work done at **Astley Hall** in the 1660s is, however, some of the most striking anywhere in the country. The house contains two remarkable plaster ceilings, which have slightly unsophisticated versions of motifs which were fashionable in London and the Home Counties before and just after the Civil War [3.13]. They were made to commemorate the marriage in 1666 of the Charnock heiress, Margaret, to Richard Brooke of Mere, who was related to the Brookes of Norton Priory, a significant Cheshire family.

The ceiling of the high, open hall, which was used as no more than an imposing entrance hall for visitors – without a lower and an upper end, which by then had little or no meaning – is divided into eight compartments by some of the beams which support the floor of the long gallery. Within these compartments there are circles or ovals, richly decorated with twisted scrolls and wreaths of flowers and fruit, which frame a rose or a cupid with his bow and arrow. Around the room runs a half-metre-deep frieze – rather like the one at the then recently-built Eltham Lodge, near London – with more scrolls and wreaths and the families' coats of arms, among which there are chubby little boys (called *putti*) playing ball. The ceiling in the single-storey drawing room to the right, which was originally the dining chamber, has scallop shells, *putti* and garlands within an oval compartment – perhaps derived from the one in the king's Banqueting House at Whitehall – even more richly

3.13. Astley Hall (Chorley): plasterwork in very high relief, dating from the 1660s and showing cupids and the coat of arms of the Brooke family, the new owners.

decorated with wreaths of flowers and fruit. These ceilings are a *tour de force* of the plasterer's craft, but perhaps not things of beauty to modern eyes.

A fine new staircase rises in what was originally a special tower to the left of the fireplace, replacing an earlier, less ornate one on the right. The newel posts, carved with 'drops' of fruit and carrying wooden vases filled with more fruit, recall the decorations in the state apartments of the Earl of Pembroke's house at Wilton near Salisbury, while the balustrades carved with rich scrolls of acanthus leaves and more *putti* call to mind similar work at Eltham Lodge.

This work at Astley Hall, with its mixture of fashionable motifs from recent Home Counties houses, was commissioned by a Cheshire gentleman and does not appear to have been followed elsewhere in Lancashire. Indeed, it appears that nothing significant was done for a generation. Then, just before the end of the seventeenth century, three major schemes – but of remodelling rather than of new building – were carried out at Levens, Hoghton and Stonyhurst.

Minor Works and Big Farmhouses

There were, of course, some relatively minor works. Most striking is the modernisation of his family's recently-bought town house in Lancaster, now known as **The Judges' Lodgings Museum** [3.14], by Thomas Cole who lived nearby at Beaumont Cote. The house, which has seven bays and three storeys above a cellar, had probably been built (or, perhaps, rebuilt) in the 1620s by Thomas Covell, a lawyer, who was also the Keeper of Lancaster Castle. It had originally an L-shaped, single-pile

3.14. The Judges' Lodgings, Lancaster: the façade, remodelled *c.*1675 to be symmetrical; its windows were originally cross-windows, as at Rufford.

plan, with a central hall with a room to either side, and the stairs and kitchen in the back wing to the left. A second rear wing appears to have been added to the right in 1675 and was linked to the left-hand wing by a corridor on two storeys behind the hall – a convenient arrangement which gave some of the advantages of the double-pile plan at less expense. The façade was also remodelled to make it fashionably symmetrical with a central doorway, and was given cross-windows as at Rufford. Only one of these is visible – blocked and high up on the left-hand gable – since the main windows now have sashes, which became fashionable around 1700.

A particular feature of Lancashire society was that there were few substantial gentry families, but a lot of small-scale freeholders and wealthy tenant farmers. This must be linked not only to the geographical fact of the relative poverty of much of the land, but also to the political fact that much of the county was either owned by the Earl of Derby, or had been owned by the Crown until it sold much of its land to many small sitting tenants in the early decades of the seventeenth century. Both before and after the Civil War, many wealthy farmers could afford for the first time to build fairly large houses – as at Carr House, near Bretherton. Many such farmers clearly aspired to be gentlemen, with the result that it is often difficult to say, from their outward form alone, whether such houses were built by poor gentlemen or wealthy farmers.

In 1635 Thomas Lister, whose descendants built Gisburne Park Hall around 1720, paid £855 – a considerable sum – to build what is now **Cromwell House** on the main street in Gisburn and proudly announced the facts on a plaque over the front door. The three-storey, four-bay house is now <u>private</u>, but was until recently the 'Ribblesdale Arms' public house. Another wealthy farmer, whose family later rose to the ranks of the gentry (by buying the Whittington estate in the 1830s), was Cornelius Greene, who in 1681 built what is now called **Slyne Manor** (a <u>private</u> house but visible from the A6). The three-storey, five-bay house [3.15] is symmetrical and no longer has the hall and cross-wings plan; it is rather like a smaller version of the Judges' Lodgings, with cross-windows, but with a back wing which gives it a T-plan. Many other parishes have similar houses, built in the 1680s and '90s by wealthy farmers who, however, failed to rise into the gentry. Basically, they never owned enough land to allow themselves to leave the house of a working farm and live solely on the rents from their tenants. One of the most interesting of such houses is **Park Hill** in Barrowford, which has a complicated history of extensions and additions until the end of the eighteenth century and is now the nucleus of the **Pendle Heritage Centre**.

In the lowland north-west of the county most such houses were built with flat fronts, as at Slyne; elsewhere they tended to have projecting, full-height gabled porches, as at Gisburn and Barrowford. There is no obvious reason to explain this. One of the last such houses is in the south-west, **Crawford Manor** (a <u>private</u> house, but visible from Manor House Drive in Crawford); it was built in 1718 by a wealthy farmer called Christopher Pennington [3.16]. Its façade is symmetrical and has a round-headed doorway and rusticated quoins, but – with its three gables and

3.15. Slyne Manor: a symmetrical front, dated 1681, with cross-windows; the house still has a single-pile plan with a rear extension.

16. Crawford Manor: the house, built in 1718, has a symmetrical front and a double-pile plan, but still has vernacular details – mullioned windows and gables.

mullion-and-transom windows – it does not look very different from Carr House at Bretherton, built a century earlier. It has, however, a double-pile plan – with two staircases at the back of the house, one for the family, the other for the servants.[10] By 1718 all gentry houses had two staircases, so that services could be provided invisibly: the family did not want to see water jugs and bed-linen, let alone coal scuttles and slop pails, in the main stairhall.

Pennington clearly had pretensions, but to be accepted as a gentleman it was no longer enough to have the biggest house in the parish; one had to count among the most important families in the hundred (one of the six subdivisions of the county) and to play some rôle at county level. Furthermore, Pennington's house stood within a working farmstead and was still built in the vernacular tradition; he would never have been accepted by the gentry as one of them. While farmers continued to build such houses for some time after 1718, gentlemen, when they came to extend or rebuild, adopted house-designs from London – which we loosely call Georgian – in order to prove and display their superior status. The several largish vernacular houses like Crawford Manor, which have survived unchanged from the decades around 1700, are the houses of farming families which failed to reach gentry status or, if they did, soon fell from it.

Commodity (and delight) at the end of the century

The first of the fashionable remodelling schemes, mentioned above, was carried out at **Levens Hall** in the early 1690s. The new owner, Colonel James Grahme, who had recently bought the house from his debt-ridden relative, Alan Bellingham, had been the Keeper of the Privy Purse to James II and was politically suspect to supporters of William III. He decided therefore to withdraw for a while to the North West and to extend his house to fit his new status as a landowner. He was a member of the powerful Graham family of Netherby in Cumberland – his elder brother owned their estates – and through his wife was related to the wealthier and more powerful Howard family in Yorkshire. He could not remodel the main façade of the house [2.16] to make it symmetrical, as fashion demanded. Instead, he closed the porch in the staircase tower at the lower end of the hall and placed the entrance doorway (with its fashionable 'shouldered' architrave) so that it led into the centre of the hall, between the great chamber on the left and the dining room on the right. (He probably also removed the Elizabethan screen.) He filled both rooms with fine furniture from London – perhaps his perquisite as a member of the previous royal household. (There are fine collections of regional seventeenth-century furniture – beds and chairs – at **Astley** and **Towneley Halls.**) Grahme also replaced the Elizabethan hall fireplace with one which had a fashionable, bulbously-curved 'bolection' surround and decorated the walls of the dining room with embossed leather. He then added a long service wing to the rear with regular rows

3.17. Hoghton Tower: a bird's-eye drawing of c.1880, showing the hall with its bay-window on the north (left) side of the upper courtyard. The apartment of c.1690 is on the first floor of the wings on the east and south sides.

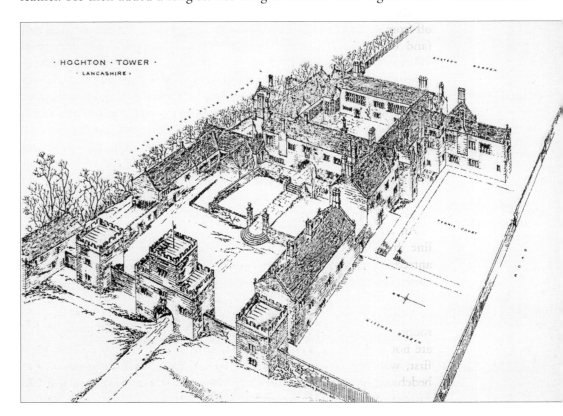

· HOGHTON · TOWER ·
· LANCASHIRE ·

of cross-windows, and in 1713 built a fine open-well staircase to supersede the Elizabethan one which, however, still rises to the left of the fireplace.

Also in the 1690s Sir Charles Hoghton remodelled the war-damaged **Hoghton Tower** after the family's fortune and finances had revived [3.17]. He repaired the house, giving the hall a fine traditional screen at the lower end with turned balusters. He then added the long wing to the right of the lower courtyard and closed this with a new castellated and centrally placed gatehouse. (He also built the magnificent Great Barn which is open to the public during the monthly farmers' markets). All this work was carried out conservatively in the traditional manner, but then within the walls around two sides of the upper courtyard he introduced, beyond the Jacobean reception rooms and at the head of a fine staircase with twisted balusters, a new and fashionable suite (or apartment) of state rooms for an honoured guest – said to have been William III, who was a friend of his.[11]

The idea of a private apartment for an important guest came from France, to which a number of courtiers and a few royalist gentlemen had been allowed by the republican government to go in voluntary exile after the Civil War. Having gone abroad, they looked around and the more intelligent of them soon realised that Britain was an 'off-shore island', cut off from the cultural centres of Europe, and that by the standards of Paris (and of Amsterdam), most English gentlemen were country cousins. When they returned to England in 1660, many of them were keen to emulate the symmetrically planned houses with a central hall and saloon and apartments, often decorated with Classical motifs, which they had admired; and they did so, as soon as their finances allowed. For a few years their models were Dutch, but soon these were replaced at the highest levels of society by even grander mansions, which people had seen in and around Paris. Charles II was half-French and had spent much of his exile at the court of his cousin, Louis XIV; French fashions soon became *de rigueur* and, trickling slowly down through the peerage, came to play a large rôle in defining the housing needs of gentry families.

An apartment was a sequence of private rooms leading in a straight line from the hall (or the saloon) of a house through a public antechamber and then a semi-public bedchamber to the very private closet (or cabinet). Many cabinets led to a back-stair, but for normal visitors an apartment was a dead-end: they went no further than the bedchamber and then had to return the way that they had come. These rooms at Hoghton could not be laid out in a straight line, however, and are not visited in the original order: the small Guinea Room, now seen first, was designed to be the closet at the end of the suite, after the bedchamber (now called the Buckingham Room). However, this is now the only surviving apartment in the county.

The rooms are panelled in the newly-fashionable simple way, in which the panels themselves are tall above a low dado – an arrangement based on the proportions of a column on its base. They are also 'raised and fielded', that is, the edges of each panel are bevelled, so that their central 'field' appears to be 'raised' or almost flush with the frame. All this panelling is now simply polished, but the Guinea Room still has some painted decorations, and other rooms had some too.

The third remodelling scheme was at **Stonyhurst** for Sir Nicholas Shireburne. Although his father had been crippled by debts and fines for recusancy, he had married well and after 1695 was able to embellish the porch under the long gallery with a pediment; in 1712 he also added tall Classical cupolas on the top of the turrets at the back of the gatehouse [2.1].

Shireburne spent much more, however, on creating the extensive gardens around the house – following French ideas to impose his mark on the wider landscape. Only a few gatepiers and a formal terrace, overlooking the Ribble valley and flanked by small gazebos with prettily swept pyramidal roofs, survive from the fine gardens on the right of the house. These were planned by Henry Wise, who was then also working at Blenheim. However, the house is approached from Hurst Green on a magnificent, long, straight avenue, bordered by two long 'canals', which were laid out by the Frenchman, Guillaume Beaumont, who had trained at Versailles and worked for James II [3.18]. When **Hoghton Tower** was repaired in the 1690s, a similar drive (but without canals) was laid out from the main road to the gatehouse; it appears in a picture of the house painted in 1735 by Arthur Devis (and which is printed in the house guide).

Levens Hall, in contrast, retains much of its garden setting, which was also designed by Beaumont. From 1694 he laid out a private garden for James Grahme to an elaborate formal plan with tall hedges, parterres

3.18. Stonyhurst: the entrance drive flanked by the two canals of 1696.

3.19. Levens Hall: some of the topiary trees which have developed from Guillaume Beaumont's French-style garden of *c.* 1690.

surrounded by box hedges and small clipped trees. (An early plan is on display in the house.) To the west of this garden the ha-ha – a boundary wall in a ditch – which prevented cattle in the surrounding meadowland from entering the garden, is considered to be the oldest example in England. (The English word comes from the French expression *Ah! Ah!* which marks not amusement, but surprise and alarm.) On the other side of the main road, which then bore little traffic, Beaumont laid out a fine long avenue of trees above the curving line of the River Kent in the deer park.

Gardens are much more difficult to conserve than buildings, because they are composed of living things and therefore change. The tall beech hedges south of Levens Hall have been well maintained for three hundred years, but the once (typically French) pyramidal trees east of the house now have exotic shapes, which would have horrified Beaumont [3.19]. Opinions vary on this matter, but my view is that Grahme's heiress, who used her childhood home as a sort of dower house after the death of her husband, the Earl of Suffolk in 1757, discouraged all changes – with the result that Beaumont's trees were left to grow unchecked in the eighteenth and early nineteenth centuries, until they were tidied up, somewhat fancifully, in Victorian times.

References

1   Francis Bacon, *Essays* – first published in 1625 and republished in 2002 by Folio Books, p. 158.

2   John Champness, 'The Building of Gawthorpe Hall' in *Contrebis*, volume 31 (2006–2007), pp. 33–41.

3   The picture is in a private collection, but can be seen in John Harris, *The Artist and the Country House* (1985), p. 219.

4   Clare Hartwell and Nikolaus Pevsner, *Lancashire: Manchester and the South East* (2004), p. 523.

5   The plan is published in W. John and Kit Smith, *An Architectural History of Towneley Hall, Burnley* (2004), p. 38.

6   Francis Bacon, *Essays*, Folio Books (2002), p 161.

7   R. T. Gunter, *The Architecture of Roger Pratt* (1928), p. 24.

8   Nicholas Cooper, *Houses of the Gentry, 1480–1680* (1999) pp. 184–5.

9   William Langland, *Piers the Ploughman,* text B, passus X, lines 97–101, (quoted in Mark Girouard, *Life in the English Country House* (1978), p. 30.

10   Richard Pollard and Nikolaus Pevsner, *Lancashire: Liverpool and the South-West* (2006), p. 164.

11   John Martin Robinson, 'Hoghton Tower, Lancashire' in *Country Life* (23 and 30 July 1992).

3.20. Levens Hall: another view of the topiary, with the house behind.

4.1. Lytham Hall: the Lodge of *c*.1870, crowned by the Clifton family's coat of arms with its crest of a sword in hand and its motto: *Mortem aut Triumphum.*

CHAPTER FOUR

Gentry Estates in the 'Golden Age' of the Long Eighteenth Century (1688–1832)

Introduction

Occasionally – although I know of no example in Lancashire – a visitor to a country house will find, hanging in the servants' quarters at the end of the tour, a large map, sometimes beautifully drawn and coloured, of the family's estate. This humble position would have surprised and saddened the builder of the house, for to gentry families the estate was all-important.

This concern is reflected in the coat of arms of the Cheetham family, which can be seen outside a few public houses in South Lancashire. The motto reads quite simply *Quod Tuum Tene*. We are used to more pretentious ones like the Cliftons' *Mortem aut Triumphum*, along with its mailed fist and sword [4.1], but here is one which bluntly says it all: hold on to what you have. A gentry family's estate was the most significant thing it possessed – more so than the house itself, which could always be rebuilt, and more so in the long run than its reputation, for the memory of a 'black sheep' would fade with time. Families went to great lengths to build up their land and enhance its value: sons were encouraged, in the words of the proverb, to live their lives as though they might die the next day, but to farm their land as though they might live for a thousand years.

The importance of a landed estate is well expressed in an article written by the fifteenth Earl of Derby in 1881. The immediate circumstance of the article was an Irish Land Act, but the article has a more general significance and could have been written in 1781 or, even, in 1681. 'The objects which men aim at when they become possessed of land,' Lord Derby wrote, 'may, I think, be enumerated as follows:

1.   political influence;
2.   social importance, founded on territorial possession, the most visible and unmistakable form of wealth;

3.   power exercised over tenantry; the pleasure of managing, directing
      and improving the estate itself;
4.   residential enjoyment, including what is called sport;
5.   the money return – the rent.'[1]

As a wealthy man with a fairly long pedigree, Lord Derby could afford to
put money last. It was, however, important to him, since the houses built
on his land near Liverpool alone had brought him a rent of £160,000 in
1876 – which would rise to £300,000 per year by 1900.[2] Even so, it would
have appeared unseemly to place money higher, since for most gentlemen
it was not the most important consideration. This was changing in the
Home Counties by 1900,[3] but as late as 1880 many newly wealthy men
were still pleased to buy estates and assume therewith the status, the
traditional trappings and responsibilities of landed families. In 1852
Thomas Miller, a Preston cotton-spinner, bought the Singleton estate
and built the church and most of the village. (His son rebuilt the Hall in
1873.) At much the same time James Darlington, a local industrialist,
built the church, school and almshouses at Charnock Richard. Even
though they will have known most of the older-established landed
families in their area for many years, it is unlikely that either man was
accepted immediately by them as an equal; their sons, though, will have
had a better chance.
     A landed estate was, quite simply, the most visible sign of a gentry
family's status. This cut both ways, since 'land taxes' – taxes levied on
the value of landed estates – were among the easiest to assess. Land was
also the main form of the gentry's wealth and the securest and
'purest'source of a family's income; it could hardly burn down or sink at
sea. Major family seats had been shown on county maps from the time of
Speed's maps in 1610, while the large-scale map which William Yates
produced in 1786 for Lancashire also marks the names of the owners.
County directories, from Pigot's 1828–9 *Commercial Directory for
Cumberland, Lancashire and Westmorland* into the early twentieth
century, list the gentry (and clergy) at the beginning of the entry for
each parish. Until the middle of the nineteenth century land was still
the source, direct or indirect, of the greatest proportion of the national
wealth and of employment. Landowners felt able to claim for this
reason, and also because they paid through land taxes a substantial
proportion of a government's tax receipts, that they should have
a large measure of political power. For a long time this claim was
accepted.
     To maintain the estate in the family was therefore a family's most
earnest endeavour. The claims of the family as a whole outweighed those
of individuals, and each holder in turn was entrusted with the family's
estates and held responsible for maintaining them intact for the heirs to

come. A number of legal devices were therefore evolved over the centuries to make this easier.

Primogeniture

The earliest in time was the practice or custom of male primogeniture, whereby the bulk of an estate was automatically transferred on the death of a father to his eldest son. There was nothing 'God-given' about the custom of primogeniture. The practice was introduced by the early Norman kings to ensure that they could rely on there being someone who would carry out the feudal duties of military service. William the Conqueror had intended to grant the major baronies anew when each tenant-in-chief died, but this became too complicated politically: sons wanted to hold on to what their fathers had held. And so it became the custom that, if the father had served the king faithfully, the eldest son inherited the whole estate by right, on the condition that he too fulfilled his obligations to the king. In due course the custom spread down the social scale from major to minor landholders, and by 1500 primogeniture was regarded as a law of Nature. It followed of course that younger sons were disadvantaged, and so special provisions were normally made for them and, of course, for their sisters. The main concern, however, was that the estate was not divided on the father's death.

Entailed Land and Strict Settlements

The second way of maintaining the link between an estate and a family was the system of entailed land and strict settlements, which was perfected in the late seventeenth century. After the government of the republican Commonwealth had put an end to all feudal practices, land was owned outright, provided that one could prove title. This continued after the Restoration, and, once the nobility and gentry had consolidated their hold on power within Parliament, they and their lawyers developed further ways of ensuring that estates were passed on intact.

In brief, these involved a legally binding agreement, normally renewed whenever an eldest son got married, that the estate or, at least, a large part of it should be 'entailed' – or settled – on specified people from three generations: the father, his son and his possible grandson. A few fields here and there could be sold off by mutual consent among neighbours to tidy up boundaries, but a large proportion of most estates – the traditional core around the family seat – was entailed; this meant that this land had to be passed on within the family and could not – until the Settled Land Act of 1882 – be sold to anyone else without a private Act of Parliament. (The eighteenth-century economist, Adam Smith, condemned the system of strict settlements, describing them – correctly – as 'a deliberate invention of the aristocracy to preserve the land in the hands of the few…at the expense of the community at large'.) Such an Act was passed in 1784 for John Dalton of Thurnham Hall and enabled him to sell his Fryerage estate in Lancaster, where Dalton Square and the surrounding streets were laid out.[4]

Before a marriage took place, a contract, called a 'settlement', was drawn up by the two families' lawyers and would be overseen later by trustees – normally the same lawyers and close friends and relations. This settlement would prescribe the legal and financial arrangements, which should underlie the marriage: it would lay down the succession, on the assumption that the marriage would produce children, but also on the off-chance that it would be childless. In his turn, the young bridegroom, on the death of his father, would become not the outright owner of the estate, but what was called the 'tenant-for-life' – the guardian of the family's landed patrimony, upon which its status depended. In addition, the settlement would make financial provision for the bridegroom's younger brothers, for his sisters, and for his wife, if she were to be widowed. (Though fair, this sometimes created problems. Alan Bellingham at Levens provides an early example. He bought the estate in 1562, knowing that the vendor's mother had the right to live in the house until she died. In the event she married again and then outlived her second husband and also Bellingham himself, so that it was his son, James, who finally moved into the house in 1578.)

There was in all of this something of a gamble. It was a question of trying to balance income and expenditure: income from rents and dowries, and outgoings in the form of the normal expenses of running a household and an estate, plus the necessity of providing for daughters' dowries, portions for younger sons and jointures for a widow. Family finances could be crippled by two closely spaced deaths of married tenants-for-life, since this would mean two sets of widows' jointures from a single income-stream. If such a case arose, other families would be wary of marrying a son or daughter into such a family while the crisis lasted.

The most striking example I know of these potential problems is that of Ralph Leycester of Toft Hall in Cheshire. He inherited the estate in 1761 and, with it, an annual income of £978, net of taxes – a sizeable sum. However, he had first to pay £286 p.a. as interest on his father's debts (largely for the purchase of property) and then £262 p.a. to finance settlements on his sisters and his seven children. This left him £430 p.a., which would have been adequate for his normal needs. However, if he were to die before his wife, she would be entitled to a widow's jointure of £403 p.a. His son would have to sell off, or mortgage, land to pay this entitlement until his mother died.[5] The Leycesters were still in possession a century later, so presumably everything worked out reasonably well.

Arrangements had also to be made for younger sons. Some of them went into the law – always useful to the family and also a lucrative profession in its own right. Some became clergymen in the Church of England, quite often in local parishes, where a friend or relative owned the advowson, or right to nominate the parson. Others were bought a commission in the army or navy. Some younger brothers – like Thomas and Andrew Stones from Much Hoole – went into some form of trade or business enterprise, with the help of a portion from the family estate and the status of a gentleman, which would give good security for their partner's loans. (It was not easy for Catholics to practise as lawyers, and impossible to secure commissions, but there is evidence that some younger sons from Catholic families became monks or priests, while daughters could become nuns.)

Marriage

The third means of ensuring the link between a family and an estate was marriage to provide a succession of legitimate male heirs. Marriage was the norm in what was a patriarchal society, and married women enjoyed a higher social status and, generally, a more comfortable lifestyle than did single women, or even widows. When a young couple marry nowadays, their parents hope first that their happiness will last a lifetime. Gentry parents before the eighteenth century almost always put happiness third behind the continuation of the family line and the enhancement of the family's acreage, wealth and social standing. However, many Georgian parents did take some care to ensure that their children were a good match on personal as well as family terms, and, if the couple were lucky, affection followed marriage.

An example which strikes a chord in modern minds is provided by Nicholas Blundell of Little Crosby. Despite the fact that he was impoverished by the outgoings demanded by the large families in the previous two generations, he wrote to his brother in 1724, 'I will not fix of any, only such as I am pretty well assured my daughters may live comfortably with, for I assure you they are deserving of good husbands... To tell me he is a Baronet's son and will have £1500 per annum will not tempt me. I value the person, parts and humours of the man (for that must make a woman happy) more than quality [= social standing].'[6] Despite all this, marriages were arranged rather like the merger of two limited companies.

The all-important link between a family and an estate was always at the mercy of the death of an heir. If a man had no surviving son, a surviving daughter, if any, would take the estate to her husband's family – as was the case when Nicholas Blundell died in 1737. This also happened twice at Levens, in 1730 and 1779. In exceptional circumstances, as at

Towneley in 1901, the estate might have to be divided between several heiresses, and, to all intents and purposes, disappeared. To be sure of surviving in the male line, a family needed in every generation to have at least as many boys as girls, and then each of those boys needed to reach adulthood and marry and produce more sons. The number of families which really have 'survived unbroken for centuries in the male line from father to son' – a myth created to enhance status through longevity – can probably be counted on the fingers of one hand.

If a man had no surviving children at all, a distant male relative would be sought to inherit the land and title – as happened at Holker in 1756, when the estate passed from the Lowthers to the Cavendishes. When the tenth Earl of Derby died without an heir in 1736, the family's lawyers had to go back to the 1450s to find a common ancestor, so that the title could pass to a distant cousin, Sir Edward Stanley, whose seat was at Bickerstaffe. When the first Earl of Wilton (formerly Sir Thomas Egerton, the builder of Heaton Hall) died in 1814, all his sons were dead. His only surviving daughter (and heiress), Eleanor, had married Robert Grosvenor of Eaton Hall near Chester, who was to become the Marquess of Westminster. In 1814 the Egerton estates were therefore added to those of the Grosvenors, but by a legal device called a Special Remainder the titles were allowed to pass to Eleanor's second son, Thomas Grosvenor, who had been born in 1799. After he had come of age in 1821, he took the name and arms of the Egertons and became the second Earl of Wilton and independent owner of the Heaton estates.

As families with less political influence than the Egertons died out, for lack of an heir, estates were combined and grew larger. Houses, which had been gentry houses and are still called Something Hall, might be used as dower houses. In this case, they would be maintained but not modernised – since no significant investment was ever made in houses which were not seats. Many survived until Victorian times – like Speke Hall or Gawthorpe Hall – as time-capsules. Some simply declined into farmhouses. Borwick Hall is an example: in 1658 it passed by marriage from the Bindloss family to the Standishes of Standish Hall, from them to the Towneleys of Towneley, then to the Stricklands of Sizergh, who sold it in 1854 to George Marton of Capernwray, who never lived there.

Daughters might delight their father's heart, but they also diminished his patrimony and, if they were heiresses, they helped to rebuild other families' houses. Occasionally, however, a husband was obliged to take the surname of his wife's family, especially if she was an heiress and a member of a well-connected family. Levens provides two examples in two generations. When Richard Bagot married the Howard heiress, Frances, in 1783, he assumed her surname, and when their daughter and heiress, Mary Howard, married Colonel Greville Upton in 1807, the couple were known as the Greville-Howards. Clearly, the name Howard counted for more in the North West than the well-regarded Midlands names of Bagot or Greville. When the doctor and high-ranking civil servant, Sir James Kay, married Janet, the heiress of the Shuttleworth family in 1842, he hyphenated his name to hers; his son, moreover, took his mother's surname as his title when he was raised to the peerage in 1902.

The value of an estate

Until the decline of arable farming in the last quarter of the nineteenth century an estate's farmland provided a generally reliable income. The home farm produced food for the 'big house' and some for the market, but it was not so important as the tenanted farms which brought in the annual rent – the 'unearned' income which guaranteed the family's status.

Most estates aimed at being more or less self-sufficient, but, as regional markets developed in the eighteenth century, thanks to improvements in transport, some estates tended to specialise in whatever they could most easily and profitably produce. Most landowners subscribed to their local County Agricultural Society, but few were innovators: many would, however, introduce new practices, when the improvement had been proven. A few – like the Cliftons of Lytham, the Gibsons of Quernmore and the Heskeths of Rufford – built model farms on parts of their estates, to teach good practice to their other tenants. A late and imposing example, dated 1846, is the square of buildings, including a boiler house and chimney, laid out symmetrically around a large courtyard at Moss House Farm by Richard Saunders, the new owner of the nearby Wennington Hall. Not all these investments bore fruit richly, however, and the Gibsons had to sell their Quernmore estate in 1842 to William Garnett, a merchant from Salford.

Responsibility for the management of the estate was normally delegated to the steward or agent, who often had an office in the big house. He was charged with optimising the commercial potential of the estate. He collected the rents each quarter at the rent table – there is a good example at Holker – and from them built or maintained roads and houses, and helped his better tenants, if they were in difficulty. Whenever he could, he also drained marshy land. This was expensive, but the use of land for arable crops could result in the doubling of its value; consequently, large-scale reclamation of the mosses and meres of the Fylde and West Lancashire as well as of the salt-marshes along the coast from Holker to Scarisbrick took place at this period.

Gentry families had other sources of income related to their ownership of land. A landowner owned the mineral deposits under his land, and this entitled him to royalties on every ton of coal, stone or other mineral extracted. Iron ore was very important in the Furness area from the late eighteenth century. Coal had been mined in the Wigan area since the

Middle Ages and provided an income for the owners of Haigh Hall, Wrightington Hall and several others. Many landowners prospected for coal, and sometimes found it in places which we would never think of: in the Lune valley there are the remains of bell-pits in a field near Aughton, and of an engine-house at Clintsfield, near Wennington. Around 1800 the owner of Hornby Castle provided coal for the poor of the parish at Christmas. Much money was, however, wasted on fruitless exploration.

Mining brought disadvantages as well as benefits: Atherton Hall was demolished in 1825, and Haigh Hall had to be rebuilt a few years later, because of the damage done to them by subsidence. Mines also brought spoil tips and subsidence flashes, noise and smoke – not to mention miners, who were often less deferential than agricultural labourers. Not a few owners moved away from South Lancashire in the nineteenth century – often to the hunting shires – but most of them retained their estates and mineral rights and consequent incomes.

A number of landowners were also fortunate enough to own land in places which might be developed on the edge of towns or as new towns. Agricultural improvements required substantial investments, but most of the first costs of urban development were paid by those who leased the building land from the landowner; he could then reap an annual reward in the form of ground rents on the houses built. Probably the first such development in Lancashire took place from 1712 at St Anne's Square in Manchester for the Mosley family, the lords of the manor. Other families owned prime sites: the Daltons of Thurnham with their Fryerage estate in Lancaster have already been mentioned, and the Earls of Stamford, whose seat was at Dunham Massey and who began to lay out the area around Stamford Street in Ashton-under-Lyne in the 1770s, are another example. We owe the quality of many of the more pleasant Victorian developments – behind the beach at Lytham and Southport, but also at Barrow (which belonged to the Dukes of Buccleugh and of Devonshire) – to the fact that they were owned by families who did not need to make a quick profit, but could afford to invest in public buildings and then control development by covenants, in the confidence – sometimes misplaced – that they would take a growing return over many years to come. More hard-headed were the Earls of Derby, who built tightly-packed terraces for dockers and railways workers in Kirkdale, as Liverpool Docks expanded in the 1870s.

Big landowners could get large-scale credit and thereby incur large-scale debts, despite the pleadings of their agents and other members of the family. Much depended, of course, on the personal qualities of individual landowners. At Lytham Thomas Clifton, the grandson of the builder of the present Hall, was something of an absentee landlord but won himself the nickname of Thomas the Tree Planter in the 1830s by planting and insisting that his tenants did so too. His son and grandson mixed more with the wealthy aristocracy, ran up large debts and were seldom seen at Lytham. Their example was well followed by Henry Talbot de Vere Clifton who inherited the estate in 1928 and managed to spend his way through three and a half millions before he died, almost penniless, in 1979.[7]

The enlargement of parks

In the lowland counties of England, where manors and townships and parishes tended to have similar boundaries, it was common in the Middle Ages and sixteenth and seventeenth centuries for manor houses to be built within a village and close to the church. We can see this at Melling, Claughton and Brookhouse in the Lune valley, and elsewhere at Leyland, Croston and Downham. This pattern was, however, fairly rare in Lancashire, where parishes were large and settlement was more scattered. Gentry houses were almost always near main roads, but tended to stand in their own parkland.

In the later eighteenth century several of these parks were enlarged, or more heavily planted, as at Lytham and Scarisbrick, so that the Hall could no longer be seen at short range and its inhabitants could enjoy a greater privacy. Sometimes – with the permission of the local JPs, of course – public roads were diverted, at the expense of the landowner, to

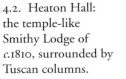

4.2. Heaton Hall: the temple-like Smithy Lodge of c.1810, surrounded by Tuscan columns.

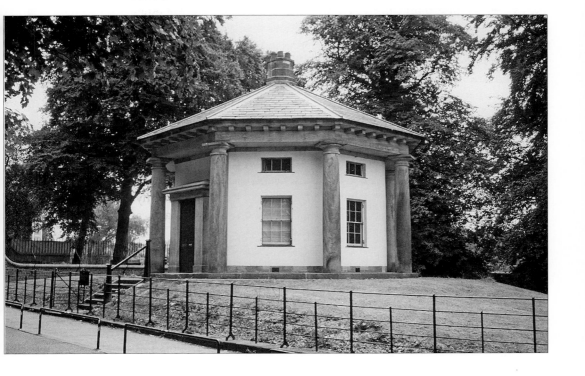

allow bigger gardens. Levens, where Ninezergh Lane was moved a little to the east in the 1690s, provides an early and small-scale example; another, a century later, is at Quernmore, where the minor road from Lancaster to Caton was re-routed – within the estate boundaries – about half a mile to the east, so that the park could be enlarged and landscaped. Heaton and Ince Blundell offer other examples, with high walls and fine gateways. A little later Lytham saw major changes to remove local roads from the vicinity of the Hall: Blackpool Road was laid out in 1832 and Ballam Road in 1845, in both cases outside the wall surrounding the park.

4.3. Gisburne Park: the Gothick lodges of c.1800 – pretty rather than impressive.

The gates at the entrance to a park were normally kept closed and were only opened by the man who lived in the lodge – which by the standards of the time was a desirable residence, often designed at the same time and in the same style as the main house. There are attractive examples at Browsholme, Lytham and Quernmore, and the finest in the county are the two at Heaton – the octagonal Smithy Lodge, ringed by eight monolithic Tuscan columns [4.2], and the monumental triumphal arch of the Grand Lodge, flanked by pairs of Doric columns. Perhaps the most striking are the tall, battlemented arch in Padiham, over the Arbory Drive to Huntroyde, and the pair of spiky Gothick pavilions at Gisburne Park [4.3].

*   *   *

Until the decline of British arable farming in the late nineteenth century, a landed estate was necessary to high political status, even though there were by then better forms of financial investment. An article in *The Economist* in 1870 put it thus: 'It would [better] pay a millionaire in England to sink half his fortune in buying 10,000 acres of land to return a shilling per cent and live on the remainder, rather than [to] live upon the whole without land. ... He would be a greater person in the eyes of more people'. And, indeed, many wealthy industrialists did buy estates with a house, or space to build one – playing the country gentleman at the weekend, while living off other sources of money. William Armstrong, the Newcastle engineer and armaments manufacturer with his house, Cragside, near Rothbury, is the best national example, but Lancashire had John Foster of Bradford's Black Dyke Mills at Hornby Castle, Harold Brocklebank of the Liverpool shipping line at Grizedale Hall, and Lord Leverhulme at Rivington.

References

1   The Earl of Derby, 'Ireland and the Land Act' in *Nineteenth Century* (October 1881) quoted in Heather A. Clemenson, *English Country Houses and Landed Estates* (1982), p. 96.

2   C. B. Phillips and J. H. Smith, *Lancashire and Cheshire from AD 1540* (1994), p. 231.

3   There are examples in J. Mordaunt Crook, *The Rise of the Nouveaux Riches* (1999).

4   There is an interesting article on this subject, entitled 'Gentlemen's Houses in Lancaster' by Andrew White, in *The Georgian Group Journal*, volume VI (1996).

5   C. B. Phillips and J. H. Smith, *Lancashire and Cheshire from AD 1540* (1994), p. 72

6   Nicholas Blundell quoted in G. E. Mingay, *The Gentry* (1976), p. 112

7   The story of the waste of this fine asset occupies most of John Kennedy, *The Clifton Chronicle* (1990). An unpublished PhD thesis (at Lancaster University) by G. Rogers, *Lancashire Landed Families* (1981) compares the Cliftons' story with that of other families.

5.1. Towneley Hall: Vassali and Quadri's classically detailed plasterwork with giant pilasters in the remodelled hall – work of *c.*1730.

CHAPTER FIVE

Gentry Houses in the Eighteenth Century

Introduction

When the story of gentry housing in Lancashire – which had been interrupted by the Civil War and its consequences – started again just before 1700, builders were eager to use designs which were already fashionable elsewhere in England – with the result that the plans, façades and interiors of their houses are similar to those being built at the same time in other parts of the country. All architects in the eighteenth century, whatever their disagreements, were fundamentally united in their belief in the supremacy of the Classical world and in the need to derive patterns for contemporary design from what they thought had been Roman practice. After a generation or so in which there had been virtually no story in Lancashire, there was then no longer a specifically Lancastrian one, but, for a century, only a national story told in this area. This chapter is, though, the longest in the book, because the Georgian period produced many of the County's finest houses, and is for me quite simply the most interesting of all because of its continuous debate on the nature of house design.

Gentry house design in the eighteenth century falls fairly neatly into two 'halves' with a break around 1760 in the matter of Commodity – a house's plan – but divides into three parts in the matter of Delight – its decoration – with breaks around 1730 and 1760. The breaks around 1760 were loosely related to each other.

In the matter of Commodity, the symmetrical plans with apartments, which had been introduced from France after the Restoration, were used until the 1750s; they were then superseded, in part as aristocratic fashion swung to a more informal style of entertaining. Within a few years of 1760 almost all newly built houses had, behind their symmetrical façades, asymmetrical plans which separated family rooms from reception rooms and allowed both visitors and family members to move easily from one room to another, without having first to pass through a centrally placed saloon. New rooms – a dining room and a library – were also introduced in the first half of the century.

In the matter of Delight, whereas an ambitious gentleman in 1700 had several London models to follow, using a wide range of Classical motifs, most architects from about 1730 accepted the stricter 'Palladian' version of Roman design. This was based on the deep understanding of Roman architecture, achieved after long study, by the Venetian architect, Andrea Palladio (1508–80), and was made fashionable by the influential third Earl of Burlington, for both the exterior and interior of houses. However, in the 1760s, as more became known about the realities of design in Roman times, this Palladian straitjacket was thrown off, and new motifs – from the Classical world, of course – were used as the basis of fashionable decoration.

Builders

The builders of most of the finest Lancashire gentry houses in the eighteenth century – like Alkrington, Croxteth, Heaton, Lytham and Towneley – were built by members of the middling or major gentry. However, the backgrounds of builders began to widen after about 1750.

Whereas Sir Thomas Bootle, the builder of the new Lathom House in the 1730s was a senior civil servant, albeit the son of a minor local gentleman, large houses began to be built from the middle of the century for men who were newly rich – not just thanks to trade, like John Carill-Worsley at Platt Hall, near Manchester (who was following an example well over a century old), but also to industry, like Thomas Patten at Bank Hall in Warrington. And this pattern was to continue, and grow, into the next century and beyond. Such new gentlemen were pleased enough to display their wealth and status but, understandably, often reluctant to use the latest fashions in the outward form of their houses; they wanted to be accepted among the gentry, but not to stand out from them.

Commodity in early Georgian Houses (*c.*1700–*c.*1730)

The first significant work in an eighteenth-century gentry house was at **Croxteth Hall**, in Croxteth Park, Liverpool, where in 1702 the fourth Viscount Molyneux extended his house by constructing a new entrance wing, built of brick with stone dressings, in front of an older house [5.2]. This set the seal on the transfer of the family seat from Sefton (where nothing now remains) to Croxteth. The Molyneux were staunchly Catholic, but clearly felt confident enough of their position in Lancashire society to build a striking house. Indeed, since the new wing, with its symmetrical plan and façade and its first use of Classical details, was by far the most up-to-date building in the county, it laid down a sort of challenge to the Earl of Derby for pre-eminence in Lancashire; it was, though, ultimately unsuccessful.

.2. Croxteth Hall:
he entrance wing of
702 was probably
he first
Classical design in
Lancashire.

The wing has a double-pile plan, but its interior was gutted by fire in
1952, so that virtually nothing remains of the fine suite of first-floor
rooms centred on the saloon, the main reception room. They were
similar to those at Hoghton Tower, but – more imposingly – arranged in
a straight line so that their doors lined up to create the fashionable
internal vista, called an 'enfilade'. This destruction was doubly
unfortunate, since no Lancashire house now shows the formal plan
introduced after the Restoration (see p. 63) with rooms placed
symmetrically on either side of the axis of the front door. In such a
house visitors in the entrance hall walked *forwards* – not, as traditionally,
to one side – most often into the saloon at the rear of the house, from
which rooms led off left and right. Sometimes there was instead a
staircase at the rear of the house, which led to the saloon above the hall,
from which rooms led off similarly. (The building which comes closest
to this arrangement is a late example – now used as Warrington Town
Hall – and is described later in this chapter.)

The façade of Croxteth Hall owed nothing to the vernacular tradition
with hall and cross-wings, but was loosely derived by its architect (who is
still unknown) from Wren's work in the 1690s at Hampton Court. It is
completely symmetrical, with eleven bays and two storeys above a service
basement, which is hidden behind a wide terrace; there are no gables, and
the roofs are virtually unseen behind a parapet. After Croxteth a
symmetrical façade was standard, but this one is more striking than
beautiful: its tall, sash-windows – an early example of the new technology
which was to become normal – are set out in an uneven rhythm, which
makes the alternation of their triangular and segmental pediments on the
main floor look uncomfortable. Similarly, the fine doorway with its

coupled Corinthian columns and open pediment proudly containing the Sefton coat of arms and military banners is rather too wide for the space available.

Fairly early in the century Roger Dicconson, a member of another long-established Catholic family, went further than Molyneux and replaced his family seat of **Wrightington Hall** [5.3], relegating the old house to be the service wing. (The house is now part of Wrightington Hospital and <u>not open to the public</u>, but it stands proudly on a low hill, and its original entrance façade can be seen from the A5209.) Dicconson's architect used another London house as his model – Sir Roger Pratt's short-lived but very influential Clarendon House on Piccadilly. The house is built of the local stone and has two tall storeys under a hipped roof, but it is only seven bays wide – plus the old house. It has, though, a double-pile plan – as all gentry houses were to do henceforth – and its outer bays project slightly, recalling somewhat the form of the traditional gentry house. The open-well staircase with its twisted balusters rises behind the original entrance hall, so the saloon was probably on the first floor over the hall.

A rare exception to this 'rule' about double-piles is **Foxdenton Hall** at Chadderton, which was built at about the same time by Alexander Radclyffe, a relative of the Radclyffes of Ordsall [5.4]. It is far from grand, but similar to Wrightington Hall with its two tall storeys and seven bays with projecting two-bay wings under hipped roofs at the front. The door leads into the centre of the hall, but this and the room above it are the only rooms in the central block. The house was built in

5.3. Wrightington Hall: the original entrance front of the house, based on a London model, the short-lived Clarendon House.

5.4. Foxdenton Hall:
a smaller version of
Wrightington Hall,
but with a single-pile
centre.

brick, but the walls of the basement, which contained the service rooms, are of stone: was the house perhaps a new one raised on largely old foundations?

Another house, which follows a common Home Counties model – four-square under a large hipped roof – is **Dallam Tower** near Milnthorpe [5.5]. (It is <u>private</u>, but visible from the public road through its park.) It was built in 1725 for Daniel Wilson, the head of an important Westmorland family and a local MP, to the designs of an as yet unknown architect. It is two storeys high above a half-hidden service basement and has a seven-bay double-pile plan with a corridor between the front and back rooms on both main floors. The spacious open well staircase rises behind the entrance hall, and the saloon is above the hall. The house was

5.5. Dallam Tower:
the original block of
1725 was based on a
common Home
Counties model; the
wings date from
c.1825.

originally built of brick, with stone pilaster strips to mark the centre and the ends, but was rendered in the 1820s, when the porte cochère and side wings were added by the Kendal architect, George Webster.

Yet another grand house of the 1720s is the central section of the <u>private</u> almshouses, now called **Bushell's Hospital** [5.6], near the church in **Goosnargh**. Its original internal layout has long since disappeared. The unknown architect designed a building of some consequence – three storeys high and (originally) nine bays wide – with a five-bay centre marked by slightly projecting corner stones, called quoins; its doorcase has Ionic columns and a pediment, and at the top is a panelled parapet, originally decorated with urns. The house became almshouses under the terms of the will of William Bushell, the vicar of Heysham, when his daughter and heiress died unmarried in 1745, but it was built as a family house by his father, a Preston woollen draper. It is therefore important as perhaps the first house to be built for a newly-rich Lancashire man in a large garden in a village, rather than in the centre of an agricultural estate.

The grandest Early Georgian house in Lancashire is **Ince Blundell Hall** [5.7], which was built around 1720 for Robert Blundell to the designs of Henry Sephton of Liverpool. Little of its original plan can be seen, and it is now a convalescent home and <u>not open to the public</u>; but it is just visible from the south-east across its parkland. The design of its façade, with nine bays and two storeys. is based on the former

5.6. Bushell's Almshouses, Goosnargh: the central nine bays, now slightly altered, were originally the country villa of a Preston merchant.

5.7. Ince Blundell
Hall: a lithograph of
1847, showing the
house of c.1720 with
its giant pilasters, and
to the right the
Pantheon of c.1800,
built to house Henry
Blundell's collection
of classical statues.

Buckingham House in London (which is now hidden within the vastly expanded Palace). Giant Corinthian pilasters at the corners – which rise across two storeys – and similar paired pilasters flanking two giant Corinthian columns in the centre, carry a prominent frieze and cornice, called an entablature, above which an attic storey half-hides the roof. All of this, coupled with the tall chimney stacks, gives a strong vertical emphasis to the façade, as at Croxteth; but the overall effect is once more rather crowded.

Delight in early Georgian Houses (*c.*1700–*c.*1730)

The most easily accessible interiors of this period are in the **Judges' Lodgings** in **Lancaster**, which was brought up-to-date in the 1720s by Edmund Cole of Beaumont Cote. The finest room on the first floor, the dining room, has been painted out in white, so that the best impression of its original décor is given by the ground-floor parlour [5.8], where the woodwork is simply polished. The panelling is divided by tall fluted pilasters, and the raised and fielded panels are fairly narrow above the prominent dado rail – much as at Hoghton Tower. Another attractive feature of the room is the cupboard opposite the windows, which contains a niche with a fashionable shell-shaped top to display the family's silver or porcelain against a grey-green background.

Plasterwork began to replace panelling as the fashionable way of decorating walls at about this time, and the finest accessible interior in an Early Georgian house is at **Towneley Hall**, where the Jacobean central block was refashioned in 1726 for Richard Towneley. On stylistic grounds, it is likely that the architect was Robert Thornton of York. The

Townleys had a house in York – at that time the 'capital' of the North of England – and they would probably have been aware of Thornton's work, for example at Beningborough Hall, designed in 1714.[1] Visitors approach the plain façade of Townley Hall across the open courtyard between the medieval tower and the early-seventeenth-century wing and then, opening a door dated 1530, unexpectedly find themselves in the middle of the long side of a high and spacious entrance hall, lined out with giant, fluted Ionic pilasters [5.1]. Above the entablature the attic storey and the ceiling are richly decorated with elaborate plasterwork. This hall replaced the earlier hall, mentioned in chapter 3, and its elaborate decoration – the original colour scheme was plain white – was carried out in 1730 by the Italian plasterers, Francesco Vassali and Martino Quadri. Their skills had been seen in Italy a few years before by gentlemen making the Grand Tour – see p. 120 – and they had been invited to work in England; they were popular because they could turn a big space into an impressive one, which suggested the power and cultural discernment of their patron.

5.8. The Judges' Lodgings, Lancaster: panelling of c.1720 in the parlour.

Such tall entrance halls were not rare in new aristocratic mansions or in the houses of ambitious gentlemen at that time – Beningborough provides an impressive example. They were probably modelled on those at Vanbrugh's recent palaces of Castle Howard and Blenheim and, perhaps, therefore, at one remove on the halls of the Middle Ages and Elizabethan England. The one at Towneley, however, is now unique in Lancashire and, with its giant pilasters, reminiscent of the façade of Ince Blundell Hall. It is certainly an imposing entrance to the house and must also have been the main room for entertaining. In the ceiling are medallion portraits of a man and a woman – perhaps of Richard Towneley and Mary his wife. Between the attic windows there are *putti* representing the four elements of earth, air, fire and water, while medallions of Roman emperors hang between the pilasters to suggest that Richard Towneley was a man of importance. The point is made again by the Towneley coat of arms with eighteen quarterings, which hangs proudly over the doorway.

Probably more noticed than the plasterwork on the ceiling are the two fireplaces, which are each framed by pairs of Ionic pilasters and decorated with a scrolled mantelshelf carrying a plaster copy of an antique statue under a canopy of drapery [5.9]. These two statues – the Medici Venus and the Dancing Faun – were popular among people who wanted to display their culture and their love of the works of the Classical world. (The relatively narrow opening of these fireplaces, when compared with earlier examples, probably means that the fuel used was coal, not wood. There were small collieries in the Burnley and Wigan areas well before 1700, and coal – burnt in an iron grate and not on the hearth – replaced wood generally in the course of the eighteenth century.)

Vassali and Quadri's bill of just over £185, paid in 1731, was expensive, but it included simpler plasterwork around a new staircase to the left of the hall. This was built on the then relatively new principle of the cantilever, where each stone tread is built firmly into the wall and is also carried on the one below it. Everything is self-supporting, and, since there are no newel posts, the staircase has an air of daring lightness, as it climbs up around the open well. This lightness is emphasised by the balustrade, which is made of elegant wrought-iron work, perhaps by Robert Bakewell of Derby.

The most lavish, and sometimes accessible, display of plasterwork from the 1730s is in the so-called **Music Room** at **Lancaster**. This was built as a summer house in the garden belonging to a house (now the private 76 Church Street) then owned by a lawyer, called Oliver Marton. (Some years previously he had bought the Capernwray estate and become thereby a gentleman.) Its three-storey façade, which displays Corinthian above Ionic pilasters, is slightly ungainly with a tall ground floor, so that people in the Music Room (on the first floor) could see the view up the Lune valley. Inside, the modelling of the plasterwork is not so refined as at Towneley [5.10]; the room

9. Towneley Hall: a plaster cast of the Medici Venus used as a chimney piece in the hall.

5.10. The Music Room, Lancaster: classical plasterwork of the 1730s – Apollo flanked by a pair of Muses.

is fairly tall, but the ensemble is somewhat overcrowded. Above the (later) fireplace stands the god Apollo with his lyre, flanked by medallions containing busts of two of the Muses, who were said to inspire artists; the other seven are in tall panels on the other walls. (It is likely that the room, and then the building, was originally called the Muses' Room.) In the ceiling is Ceres the goddess of agriculture, surrounded by garlands of fruit and flowers and medallions bearing portraits of Roman emperors and trophies of arms – to suggest that Marton was a cultivated and wealthy landowner.

Commodity in Palladian Houses (c.1730–c.1760)

What is noticeable about the Early Georgian houses, mentioned above, is the variety of their façades, their plans and their interior decoration. Much of this variety was to disappear for about thirty years, once Palladian design principles became more or less standard, thanks to the influence of the third Earl of Burlington. (Most art-historical terms, like 'Gothic' or 'Baroque', were not invented until the nineteenth centuries and were often used as terms of abuse, but 'Palladian' was a term used widely in Georgian England and in a complimentary sense.)

The Palladian manner was in many ways no more than the house style of the 'Whig oligarchy', the group of peers who dominated British politics between 1715 and 1760. It therefore characterised the architecture of their palatial houses in the Home Counties and neighbouring shires, where most of them had their seats; but it played a lesser role in gentry house building in the North Midlands and Lancashire. Nevertheless, although its ascendancy lasted little more than a generation, it was important as a reaction to the major buildings of the recent past, and also of lasting importance into the future.

It takes some effort to understand the driving force behind Palladian theory and practice in Britain, but with hindsight we can see that Palladian design was part of a Western European reaction of taste in the first half of the eighteenth century from more complicated and sometimes extravagant Classical designs (now often called Baroque) to simpler and more restrained work. In Britain, however, this more or less natural reaction was exaggerated – and exacerbated – by politics, Protestantism and anti-French feeling. We need to see it against the background of Britain's victory in 1714 after a generation-long war against Louis XIV's France. This was followed in the same year by the accession of the Protestant Hanoverian king, George I, who chose most of his ministers among Whig politicians (who were anti-French and therefore anti-Catholic), and then by the defeat in 1715 of the Jacobites' attempt, with French help, to place a Catholic king on the throne of Great Britain in the place of George.

To over-simplify a very complicated story: even though for fifty years France had been regarded almost everywhere in Europe as the continent's cultural centre, Whig leaders felt that a victorious Britain needed a serious and noble national style of architecture, which should, of course, be inspired by the example of ancient Rome, but not based on French (and therefore also Catholic) models. What then should they do? As educated Britons did, they regarded themselves as latter-day Romans and came to believe that the best way forward was to put the clock back and follow the example set by the English architect, Inigo Jones, before the Civil War. Jones had been to Italy in the early 1600s to study the buildings and the books of Palladio, who had died some twenty years before. He had been very impressed by Palladio's understanding and interpretation of the achievements of Roman architecture and, after his return, had followed the example of Palladio's restrained designs in a few simple, well-proportioned (but, inside, richly decorated) buildings for the royal family – notably the Banqueting House in Whitehall and the Queen's House at Greenwich. If the Civil War had not broken out, they would doubtless have been widely emulated in the 1640s and '50s. The Whigs believed furthermore that, without the war, Jones' buildings, rather than French palaces, would have been the basis for English gentry-house design in the later seventeenth century.

There was already some interest in Palladio by 1700, both on the Continent and in England. In 1715 a Venetian architect, Giacomo Leoni, who had come to work in England, published a translation (illustrated with his own engravings) of Palladio's comprehensive treatise, *Four Books on Architecture;* and in the same year a Scottish architect, Colen Campbell, produced the first volume of his *Vitruvius Britannicus.* This was not a work of history but of discreet self-publicity, containing 100 fine engravings of impressive recent English houses, among which was the palatial Wanstead House near London which Campbell had just designed. Campbell's implication was that a better future for British architecture would be ensured if, once again, people were to follow the example of Inigo Jones, whom he nicknamed 'the British Vitruvius' – after the Roman architect who lived just before the time of Christ and who was regarded in the eighteenth century as the main authority on Classical architecture. Campbell had followed Jones' ideas at Wanstead and could, he implied, do it again for anyone who wished to commission him. Wanstead House soon became the model for a seat for noble families or for wealthy gentry – a 'house of parade', as people said. (It was demolished in 1824.) In 1721 Campbell went on to design a U-shaped 'villa' or smaller gentry house at Stourhead (near Frome in Somerset); it is five bays wide by nine bays deep and still survives. This later provided the pattern for many Georgian gentry houses – especially in an extended form with wings to the sides, which I shall call the 'villa-plus' plan and which became fashionable around 1750.

Meanwhile, in 1716 Lord Burlington, who was a prominent Whig, commissioned Campbell to teach him about Jones and Palladio and also to remodel his London home, Burlington House on Piccadilly – now the home of the Royal Academy. This led him to make a short visit to North Italy to see with his own eyes houses designed by Palladio; and after this he too came to believe that Palladio's approach to house-design provided the best model to follow. In practice this involved little more than placing the main reception rooms prominently on the first floor above a clearly visible basement, and not on the ground floor a few steps above a half-hidden service basement, as had been current in France and therefore in England for a century; Dallam Tower is a good example. It was thus a significant – and anti-French – change, also symbolised by the fact that Palladians liked to use the Italian term *il piano nobile* for the main floor. (In Palladio's country houses, often built on the extensive, flat plain of the River Po, the basement had been used for storage and to protect the fine rooms of the *piano nobile* from rising damp; in England it was used for family and service rooms.) In the matter of decoration Burlington advocated the use of the Classical motifs and the proportions for windows and columns which Palladio had shown in his *Four Books.* He was convinced that arrangements which looked well and worked well in Italy would also look well and work well in England: in short, that the only way for self-respecting Whig gentlemen to design buildings was in the Palladian manner. He was soon to do this himself, and to do it well.

Burlington then pushed competent and compliant craftsmen and designers – and compliance was the only sensible approach for them in an aristocratic society – into positions in the government's Office of Works, which he more or less controlled until 1733. This in effect created a sort of dictatorship of the only 'correct' taste: not to follow this came to be regarded almost as a form of bad manners. Palladio's design principles, and the formulae for proportions which would produce 'perfect' solutions, especially for façades but also for internal spaces, were thereafter widely propagated by built examples, and also by pattern books for the use of provincial craftsmen and aspiring architects.

Burlington's approach can be well seen in an Early Victorian print [5.11] showing the grandest (and perhaps also the first) Palladian house in Lancashire – **Lathom House**, which was built to the designs of Giacomo Leoni in the later 1730s. (It is likely that he was introduced to Lancashire by Peter Legh of Lyme Park, near Stockport, for whom he had recently designed the south front, the inner courtyard and several fine rooms.) Lathom House stood on the site of the Earl of Derby's famous house, near Ormskirk, which had been badly damaged after two sieges in the Civil War and was later demolished. Knowsley thereafter became the Derbys' principal seat, and the Lathom estate was sold in 1724 to Thomas Bootle, who built the house illustrated here. He was a lawyer from a gentry family nearby in Melling, one of the MPs for Liverpool and chancellor to Frederick, the Prince of Wales. His almost palatial house was built for a man who hoped soon to achieve high political office; he was knighted in 1746, but Prince Frederick died before his father in 1751.

Every building in the print apart from the stable block on the right, which has recently been converted into flats, was demolished either in 1929 or 1960. (It was while I was preparing an abortive scheme for converting this stable block in 1979 that I came across a well, lined with thin bricks; I surmised then that this was the site of the Derbys' old house, and this was proved by proper archaeological excavations in 2001.)

1. Lathom Hall: a lithograph of 1847 showing Leoni's design of c.1730 – the grandest and perhaps the first Palladian house in Lancashire.

Between the stables and the matching pavilion on the left – which gave the house the plan of a large 'villa-plus' – the entrance front of Lathom's main block had nine bays; its three-bay centre and outermost bays projected slightly and were emphasised by quoins. Three features of the façade set it apart from any earlier gentry house in Lancashire. Most noticeable was the prominent pediment which rises above the centre of the roof. This feature, derived from the gable of the façade of a Roman temple, was believed by Palladio – but wrongly – to have been used on the houses of Roman nobles; it soon became a hallmark of Palladian design. Used primarily as a status symbol, it gives a good deal of emphasis to the centre of a façade – too much, perhaps, unless it is countered, as in this case, by some emphasis on the ends.

The second novelty was the ground floor, in which the masonry was 'rusticated' – with deeply cut joints between the stones, which make the wall appear more rugged and therefore more solid. This stresses the smoothness of the stone on the main floor and also changes the proportions of the façade by placing more emphasis on its horizontal divisions. Instead of two storeys of tall windows above a half-hidden basement, as at Wrightington or Dallam – an arrangement which emphasises the vertical links between the storeys – the Palladian façade with its fairly low ground floor, which serves as a plinth for the markedly taller first floor, and with a low second floor for bedchambers, appears to have three layers of windows. (Historians call this arrangement 'two and a half storeys'.)

Thirdly, the space between the windows is wider than the windows themselves, which again gives a horizontal emphasis. All these windows were, of course, carefully proportioned: whereas those on the top floor were square, those on the *piano nobile* were about 1½ times as high as they are wide. (The ideal proportion was 1: 1.414 or the square root of 2, which could be easily drawn with compasses and had an almost mystical significance for Palladians – as, indeed, it had had in Renaissance times, in the Middle Ages and earlier.) Lord Burlington would have applauded this design, since it followed the pattern of most of Palladio's palaces and country houses in North Italy.

The Victorian print shows a double staircase leading to a glazed entrance door on the first floor, but plans of 1767 suggest that the original entrance was in the rusticated ground floor,[2] where a fairly low, vaulted room – called the Sub Hall – supported the main hall on the *piano nobile*, which was reached by two spacious open-well staircases inside the house. This main hall must have been a very impressive space, since it was as high as the hall at Towneley but somewhat larger in area. Beyond the hall, which was probably the main reception room, was the smaller saloon, from which a number of other rooms led off symmetrically to either side; some were private, two-room apartments.

(The layout of reception rooms on a Palladian *piano nobile* was normally the same 'formal' one which had long been usual in major houses.)

At about the same time Leoni also designed **Alkrington Hall**, near Middleton (which is now <u>private</u> flats), when Darcy Lever commissioned him to rebuild his family seat on its site on the top of a hill [5.12]. His restrained design – it is dated 1735 – has considerable power and elegance. The brick-built nine-bay façade has two and a half storeys, but no pediment; instead, the three-bay centre is framed by giant Ionic pilasters of stone, and only the centre of the ground floor is rusticated. The result is that, although the house has low side-pavilions – which are probably not the original ones – the façade has a greater vertical emphasis than is common in most Palladian houses in England. (Perhaps Leoni, as a 'modern' Italian, stood less in awe of Palladio than did Burlington.) The entrance hall is the largest room on the ground floor; doors on either side towards the back lead to open-well staircases – the finer on the right – each lit by a tall, round-headed window. The first-floor plan is similar, so it is probable that the room above the hall, which has the most elaborate windows on the façade, was the saloon.

A grander Palladian façade – this time with four Ionic columns carrying the central pediment, which is the most usual Palladian format – is at **Allerton Hall**, Liverpool [5.13], which is now a public house. It was begun in the 1740s for two Rochdale merchants, John and James Hardman, to replace the old manor house on the estate, which they had recently bought; they must have hoped thereby to set the seal on their rise into the gentry. Both men died soon after, however, and the house was not finished until 1812; for sixty years the centre and right half of the

5.12. Alkrington Hall: the more restrained but dignified Palladian entrance façade of another house by Leoni.

5.13. Allerton Hall: almost a Palladian house of parade, but with a ground-floor entrance. It was built for a wealthy businessman.

façade simply stood against the old house. Whoever the architect was, he produced an imposing design – almost a house of parade – built of the local red sandstone, two and a half storeys high and eleven bays wide. Its ground floor, where the entrance doorway stands, is rusticated, but the outer two bays on each side project slightly, increasing the vertical emphasis within the wide façade and thus countering the emphasis of the centre with its columns. The more ornate windows suggest that the saloon was above the front entrance, but the interior was twice badly damaged by fire in the 1990s and is now of little interest.

The grandest Palladian house surviving in the county, and also the finest of the several houses built for Lancashire businessmen, is now **Warrington Town Hall** [5.14]. Originally called **Bank Hall**, it was a suburban mansion with the 'villa-plus' plan of a central block and detached side wings; it was designed by the London architect, James Gibbs, for Thomas Patten and finished in 1750. Patten's father had been a promoter of the scheme to improve the channel of the River Mersey up to Warrington and had opened a copper-smelting works nearby at Bank Quay in 1717.[3] His son bought an estate at Winmarleigh near Garstang (for the shooting) and was soon regarded as a gentleman.

The main house is built of brick, though the lowest courses of the internal walls of the basement are constructed of large blocks of copper slag. The three slightly-projecting central bays of the nine-bay entrance front are clad to their full height with rusticated stonework and have four columns of the Composite order to carry the pediment, which displays the Patten family's coat of arms. The ground floor is similarly rusticated and forms the basement of the *piano nobile*; it also extends slightly beyond the main house, which reduces the emphasis of the centre. The main entrance to the house has to be reached up a fine double flight of

14. Warrington Town Hall (formerly Bank Hall): Palladian grandeur – for an industrialist – with the ntrance on the first floor, the *piano nobile*. There is also a service wing to each side.

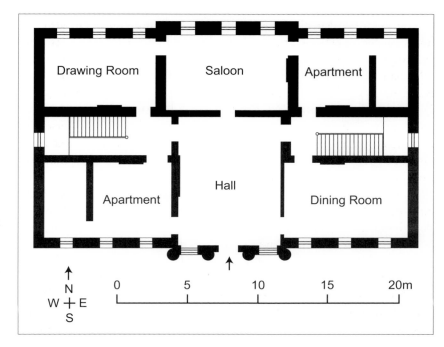

15. Warrington own Hall: the ymmetrical plan has ne hall and saloon in ne, with the rawing room to the ft of the saloon and a apartment to the ght, and a ymmetrical pair of aircases.

external stairs. The round-headed windows of the entrance hall have what are called 'Gibbs surrounds' – in which the stones are alternately shaped as parts of a normal architrave or left as square blocks.

The plan of the interior [5.15] is symmetrical and still has the formal arrangement, but its layout has been slightly modified. The entrance hall on the *piano nobile* leads to the smaller saloon on the same axis. The hall is not particularly tall, but is the largest room in the house and must have been used as the main reception room. The former saloon has been extended into what was originally the drawing room on the left; on the right were two rooms which formed a small private apartment, probably for a member of the family. On either side of the hall, as at Alkrington, is a door leading to one of two open-well staircases with an elegant wrought-iron balustrade; the finer one on the left only links the *piano nobile* to the chamber floor above, but the plainer one on the right, which was used by servants, leads up to the attics and also down to the basement. While the house is three rooms wide, as had traditionally been the case, the stairhalls divide it into (more or less) three spaces from front to back. By 1750 this was becoming normal, and by the end of the century many houses were in fact not merely double-pile houses, but triple-pile houses; Heaton Hall is a good example.

Delight in Palladian Houses (*c.*1730–*c.*1760)

The interior of Allerton Hall has been badly damaged, and Warrington Town Hall is seldom open to visitors, so that the best place to gain an impression of a Palladian house – inside and out – is **Platt Hall** in **Manchester**, now used as a museum of costume [5.16]. It was built of brick for a wealthy textile merchant, John Carill-Worsley, who had

5.16. Platt Hall: a Palladian house for an industrialist with a 'villa-plus' façade, but with a ground-floor entrance.

married the heiress of the Platt estate and taken her surname. A design was produced for him in 1761 by the York architect, John Carr, who had been clerk of works for Lord Burlington at a house which the latter had designed near York and therefore knew how to design in the Palladian manner. It was, however, modified in 1762 by another architect, Timothy Lightoler, and was finished in 1764.[4] Its two-and-a-half-storey façade is somewhat plain: it has a pediment without columns, but the entrance on the ground floor is emphasised by a single-storey portico carried on four Ionic columns. The house is fairly small – only seven bays wide – but it has the 'villa-plus' plan with wings and pavilions, for stables on the right and the kitchen on the left.

A similar, but smaller house – its centre has only five bays – can be seen across its park at Broughton Lodge, near Cartmel. (It is private.) It was built around 1780 for another industrialist, Josiah Birch, the director of the cotton mill at Backbarrow.[5] This Palladian format for country houses continued to be the model for most buildings of significance in the second half of the eighteenth century, wherever a noble and restrained character was necessary. A good example can be seen in the central block, screen walls and side pavilions which form the **Bridge Houses** at **Lancaster** and which were designed in 1786 by Thomas Harrison as part of his scheme for Skerton Bridge.[6]

Some of the interior at Platt Hall is still intact. The finest room is the dining room which is, of course, on the first floor; its central window with its pediment and ornamental surround can be seen above the front door. The approach to it is quite impressive – at first there is the low but wide ground-floor vestibule, decorated with two pairs of Ionic columns, and then, in a very attractive stairhall, designed by Lightoler, the visitor rises into the light up either flight of a curved cantilevered staircase with a wrought-iron balustrade of lyre-shaped panels. (This is in effect a small-scale 'imperial staircase' – rising up in a single flight to the half-landing, from which two flights then rise in the opposite direction up the side walls. Carr had suggested such a staircase with straight flights and a bay window at the half-landing, but Lightoler's curved flights were preferred by Carrill-Worsley. It is easy to see why.) At the top is another screen of columns – Corinthian ones this time [5.17]. The major doorcases are also framed by Corinthian columns and pediments. (When the rules of Classical design were first reformulated in Renaissance Italy, no one had seen the interior of a Roman house. The assumption was made that Roman interiors had been decorated in much the same way as exteriors – as had been the case in the Middle Ages – and so external features, like columns and pediments, were used inside to decorate doorcases, panelling and even chimneypieces – although the Romans did not have fireplaces. Palladian architects followed the same conventions, but after the 1760s most doors were framed by simple architraves.)

The dining room at Platt Hall is decorated with plasterwork, designed by Lightoler, which reflects the changing taste in interior decoration away from Palladian formality and restraint. This more relaxed work is based on motifs of slightly asymmetrical but balanced scrolls of acanthus leaves in fairly high relief and in the shape of a long C or a lazy S – which go by the name of Rococo work. (There is a little such work in the saloon ceiling and on the staircase walls at Warrington Town Hall.) At Platt it includes the frame of an attractive landscape, painted by Richard Wilson – still in its original position, as a chimneypiece above the fireplace [5.18]. The mid-blue colour scheme is the original one. The mantelshelf is carried on a pair of Ionic columns, and the frame above it is decorated with vine trails and grapes which suggest the main use of the room. This is an early example in Lancashire of the single-purpose dining room, introduced to replace the multi-purpose saloon; nevertheless, since it is a fairly small room, people probably sat to eat at small gate-leg tables, brought out when necessary. (Nationally, the earliest example of a dining room is considered to be at Houghton Hall, in Norfolk, built in the 1720s.)

5.17. Platt Hall: the top of the centrally placed stair-hall, with its Corinthian details and a view into the dining room.

After the introduction of dining rooms, saloons – which had developed from great chambers – reverted to their original function as reception rooms for socialising. They soon became the rooms to which the women withdrew after dinner to make tea or coffee and chat, before the men, who sat drinking somewhat longer in the dining room, joined them. Their name was changed in time to 'drawing room', and they tended to be considered, and even decorated, as 'feminine' rooms. This contrast is beautifully visible in the drawing room and dining room in the (private) house on Belle Isle, Windermere, recently restored after a serious fire: the drawing room ceiling has elegant and delicate plasterwork, whereas the frieze below the ceiling in the dining room is decorated with fox-heads. (In the 1760s dinner, the main meal of the day, was eaten at about 2pm, but dinner-time got progressively later until,

5.18. Platt Hall: the Rococo chimneypiece in the dining room, forming the frame to a specially painted landscape.

around 1900, it was at about 8pm; the gap between it and breakfast was by then filled by luncheon around 1pm and tea at five o' clock.)

Commodity in later Georgian Houses (*c*.1760–*c*.1800)

Almost as grand from the outside as Warrington Town Hall is **Lytham Hall**, which is the finest Mid-Georgian house in Lancashire [front cover and 5.19]. It was built of brick between 1757 and 1764 to the designs of John Carr in front of a probably Jacobean house, which will have been embarrassingly old-fashioned for an ambitious young man like its owner, Thomas Clifton. It may look like a textbook Palladian house with its nine bays, two and a half storeys with Gibbs surrounds to the ground-floor windows, and four Ionic columns carrying a pediment, but this is deceptive and, for that reason, important: the house sits, as it were, on the cusp of a significant development. Its plan is no longer the normal symmetrical one with rooms leading off a central saloon; furthermore, the main reception rooms are on the ground floor and not on the floor above. Both changes had arisen recently – but independently – after the fashionable way of aristocratic entertaining changed, and when people came to learn more about what Roman architecture had really been like.

What made the symmetrical plan unsatisfactory were changes in the fashions for receiving guests in aristocratic houses. In brief, entertaining was becoming more informal under the influence of fashionable assemblies at Bath, Buxton and other spas; here, instead of a meal being followed by, say, cards and then dancing, people could choose what they wanted to do at any time and in any order, because everything was available at the same time – thanks to the invention of the 'circuit', in which all rooms were interconnected. The first such designs for private houses, rather than public assembly rooms, were worked out in aristocratic suburban villas like **Marble Hill**, built in 1729 on the bank of

5.19. Lytham Hall: an almost-Palladian façade, hiding the fact that the reception rooms are on the ground floor.

the Thames near Twickenham; here space was tight behind a five-bay façade, but all the major rooms were needed. The solution at Marble Hill was to remove the dead ends, imposed by a symmetrical plan, and to place the main stairhall against one wall of the house (the pattern later followed at Lytham) and to link it to the rooms on either side. Another way – only possible in a larger house – was to place the main stairs in the centre of the building under a skylight; such an idea (which was to be used at Heaton Hall) was used in the 1740s by James Paine for both staircases at **Nostell Priory**, near Wakefield, and soon received aristocratic approval.

The final accolade for a more flexible and asymmetrical layout was given in 1756, when the Duke and Duchess of Norfolk introduced in their London house on St James' Square – an otherwise typically Palladian mansion – a circuit of state rooms on the *piano nobile*, leading visitors from an antechamber at the head of the centrally-placed stairs through a succession of reception rooms to a bedchamber, and then back to the antechamber.[7] (Norfolk House was demolished in 1937, but the Music Room of the suite, richly decorated in gold on white, can be seen at the Victoria and Albert Museum in London.) Thereafter the circuit plan was soon generalised – though without a state bedchamber in the houses of mere gentlemen – and it, or something similar, remained in use until the late nineteenth century; it was quite simply more convenient both for daily life and for formal receptions.

Under the new arrangement a house's plan was asymmetrical: instead of going straight on to the saloon on the *piano nobile*, as had been done earlier in the century, visitors in new gentry houses normally went *either to the right or to the left* from the entrance hall to the reception rooms, leaving the family's everyday rooms on the other side of the hall. Most reception rooms were placed on the south side of the house, if possible, to benefit from the sunlight, but the use of an asymmetrical plan meant that the entrance to the house did not necessarily have to be on the south. Greater flexibility became possible.

At about the same time the cross-section of houses was beginning to change. People were coming to see that reception rooms on the first floor had practical disadvantages – though they did give good views of gardens. For a time the disadvantages were overlooked, because the *piano nobile* enjoyed aristocratic patronage; but Burlington had died in 1753, and before then scholars were learning that wealthy Romans had lived in houses with no more than a single storey. People soon realised that Palladian precepts were not in fact based on an accurate description of Roman architecture and, therefore, did not need to be followed to the letter. In consequence, reception rooms were brought down to the ground floor, and bedrooms (and their dressing rooms) were placed on the upper floor; service rooms, which had been on the ground floor, had to go elsewhere; one possible place was to the rear of the house.

All of this can be seen in the plan of **Lytham Hall** [5.20]. Although the east-facing façade with its giant columns and pediment suggests that the

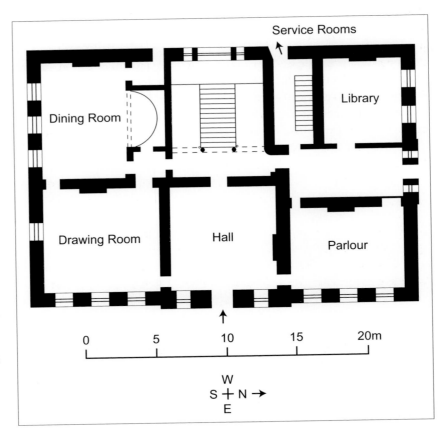

5.20. Lytham Hall: the new-style asymmetrical plan with the side-lit stair-hall behind the hall, but with reception rooms on the left and family rooms on the right. (The names of the rooms come from a plan, probably drawn *c.*1760 and now in the Gillow archives.)

reception rooms are symmetrically placed on the first floor, they are in fact on the ground floor, and on the south (or left) of the entrance hall. On most days, however, the Cliftons and people coming on business would have entered the house through the door on the right-hand (or north) side of the house, which gives access to a wide vestibule; on the left of this is the 'common sitting parlour' – the family's living room – and, on the right, the 'library' – probably the owner's study – whose panelling with tall Ionic pilasters must have been brought from the old house. The service staircase adjoins the vestibule, and the service rooms stand around a courtyard at the back; they were formed, at least in part, from the old house. Such an arrangement was not uncommon: the old house could remain in use while the new one was being built. Other new Georgian houses, built in front of older ones which were thereafter used as service rooms, can be seen at Cuerden, Kirkland, Knuzden and Rivington Halls. (All are <u>private</u> houses.) By 1800, though, almost all new gentry houses were designed to replace an older house completely.

Carr's most impressive house in our area is **Tabley House** in Cheshire, which he designed in 1761 for a wealthy baronet, Sir Peter Byrne Leicester. He was Irish by birth and had inherited his English title though his mother as a boy, so he was perhaps a little diffident. He chose a safely conservative design which – hindsight tells us – was becoming old-fashioned [5.21]. It has the full Palladian arrangement of house and wings (to the rear), a façade of two and a half storeys with a low rusticated ground floor, and a tall *piano nobile*. The main entrance is under a projecting Doric portico (which gives good views over the flat landscape); it has a pediment and coat of arms, and is approached up a pair of external staircases. Inside, the plan was originally more or less

5.21. Tabley House: grander than Lytham with its projecting portico and wings, but on the point of becoming old-fashioned.

symmetrical, but much of its original interior decoration, which was finished in 1767, that is, after Lytham, is more up-to-date than at Lytham.

Thomas Clifton, the builder of Lytham, was a man in his thirties, who rightly considered himself to be the most important landowner in the Fylde. Having recently married the daughter of an earl, he needed a finer and more modern house and, though he was a Catholic, he clearly felt no qualms about building ostentatiously only ten years or so after the failed Jacobite rising of 1745. The entrance doorway is emphasised by Doric columns carrying a full entablature and a pediment; it leads to a fairly low but imposing hall, where the main doorcases are given Doric columns and pediments to match those of the front door. The rest of the decoration consists of luxurious Rococo plasterwork [5.22] and is concentrated on and above the fireplace, which like many fireplaces in Palladian houses is integrated with a tall chimneypiece.

From the hall visitors walk across a one-sided corridor, which is connected by doors to the other important ground-floor rooms. A pair of Ionic columns half-screen it from the magnificent stairhall [5.23], which is more than twice as high and opens up immediately. The timber staircase, with three turned and richly carved balusters per tread, is an imperial staircase. It was designed before the one at Platt and was probably the first in Lancashire – perhaps inspired by the staircase at James Paine's recent Mansion House in Doncaster, which Carr, as a Yorkshireman, must have known. Such splendid staircases need a lot of space, because their plan is symmetrical, and at Lytham the stairhall is the biggest room in the house. The imposing space is lit from a 'Venetian' window, in which the central one of the three lights is taller and has a round head. The walls are decorated with plaster panels,

5.22. Lytham Hall: the rich Rococo plasterwork of the hall with the stair-hall beyond the Doric doorcase.

of which four contain Rococo 'drops', modelled in high relief and representing field sports and the arts – the ideal pursuits of a country gentleman.

The coved ceiling of the stairhall frames a relief of Jupiter, the king of the Roman gods, standing majestically on the clouds of heaven, accompanied by an eagle and carrying a sceptre and a brace of thunderbolts [5.24]. Thomas Clifton did not believe in Jupiter any more than we do, but Jupiter was a symbol of great power, well used: he was the creator and sustainer of the universe, the upholder of the moral order and the punisher of wicked men. Clifton was no doubt flattered by the suggestion from Carr's Italian plasterer, Giuseppe Cortese, that this was a suitable motif for the finest space in the house, for he and his father had created fine farmland by the draining of Lytham Moss, and he was the most powerful man in the Fylde and responsible for the lawful behaviour of the Catholic community.

5.23. Lytham Hall: the stair-hall, with its Ionic columns on the ground floor and Corinthian columns above, and Rococo plasterwork depicting shooting.

5.24. Lytham Hall: Rococo plasterwork framing the bas-relief of Jupiter above the stair-hall – an allusion to the power in the Fylde of the Clifton family.

5.25. Lytham Hall: the bed-alcove in what was originally the Cliftons' bedroom.

At the top of the stairs, another pair of columns – this time Corinthian columns which match those in the Venetian window – define a corridor leading to the main bedrooms. These bedrooms were private rooms, and so – it seems strange with hindsight – at the very moment when the finest form of staircase had been introduced, the stairhall was no longer used, as at Platt Hall, as the grand ceremonial way up to the main reception rooms (since these were on the ground floor) but was simply a fine space for visitors to admire from below or, perhaps, from the half-landing. The Cliftons will doubtless have enjoyed it every day, since they had a large apartment on the right-hand side of the head of the stairs. The most prettily decorated room there must have been Mrs Clifton's boudoir. The couple's bedroom was in the front corner of the house [5.25], where it still retains the special bed-alcove, framed with Doric columns, with a small room on either side where clothes and, probably, a close stool were stored. (The room on the right is now a 1930s bathroom – a real period piece.)

The dining room and drawing room, which would have been used by both the family and visitors, are downstairs on the left of the hall (with which they and the stairhall formed a circuit.) They were redecorated to be fashionable in the 1790s (see later on p. 121), and the house remains to this day a Mid/Late-Georgian time-capsule, because after 1800 the Cliftons became increasingly wealthy and, with it, increasingly absentee landlords; in consequence, their house was hardly modernised.

Before then the most important Late Georgian house in Lancashire – and, without doubt, one of the finest in the whole country – had been built at **Heaton Hall**. It was the work of two ambitious young men who clearly must have wanted to be at the forefront of fashion. They were the 23–year-old owner, Sir Thomas Egerton, who had recently inherited the large farming and mining estate north of Manchester, and his architect, the 26–year-old James Wyatt, whom Egerton had got to know through his wife's relations at Kedleston Hall in Derbyshire. Wyatt was then enjoying the success which had accompanied the opening of his beautiful and spacious Pantheon assembly room in London and was regarded by many as the up-and-coming fashionable architect and rival to Robert Adam, the most ambitious of contemporary designers – who, however, designed nothing significant in Lancashire.

Egerton had inherited a fairly recent Palladian house about as large as Lytham Hall. Between 1772 and 1776 Wyatt replaced it with a stone-faced, two-storey house above cellars. Once reception rooms were on the ground floor, there was no need for a third storey, and most houses were built with a two-storey cross-section. Such a house was Leighton Hall [back cover] which was built with a symmetrical plan above cellars c.1760 and given a Gothic skin in the early 1820s. (Haigh and Holker were, admittedly, built as three-storey houses in the earlier-nineteenth century, but probably because they were linked to older houses.)

At Heaton Wyatt also cleverly contrived a new, and deeper, plan [5.26]. On the ground floor there is an entrance hall with apsidal ends, which is wider than it is deep. Visitors then pass across the front of the spacious, top-lit stairhall, beyond which extends a south-facing suite of three exquisitely decorated reception rooms, which present a strong contrast to the severity of the hall. The beautiful saloon with its graceful bow-window is placed between the dining room and the drawing room. This latter is now called the billiards room, but this cannot be the original name, since all the paintings in the room (which were produced for it and fixed to the walls) have themes which one could loosely describe as 'feminine'.[8] A pair of approximately Corinthian columns separate it from a one-sided, barrel-vaulted corridor which links all the rooms and emphasizes the long enfilade from the dining room to the (slightly later) music room. The latter lies within one of the extensive wings which lead left and right into pavilions. The family's private rooms were just beyond the dining room.

Delight in later Georgian Houses (c.1760–c.1800)

Outside Court and Whig circles Palladian principles were never universally accepted as the only way of designing houses and other buildings of quality. To an extent they bore the seeds of their own decay, since they were based on a serious attempt to go back to the origins of Classical design – even beyond Palladio and the Italian Renaissance – and to use these as the basis of contemporary work. In time the question arose: how far back should one go? This became more urgent in the middle of the eighteenth century, since discoveries were being made by scholars on Roman sites, not only at Herculaneum and Pompeii, near Naples (which had been engulfed in volcanic débris after the eruption of Vesuvius in 79 AD), but also above ground in places like Split in Croatia and Palmyra in Syria (both then part of the Ottoman empire, but just

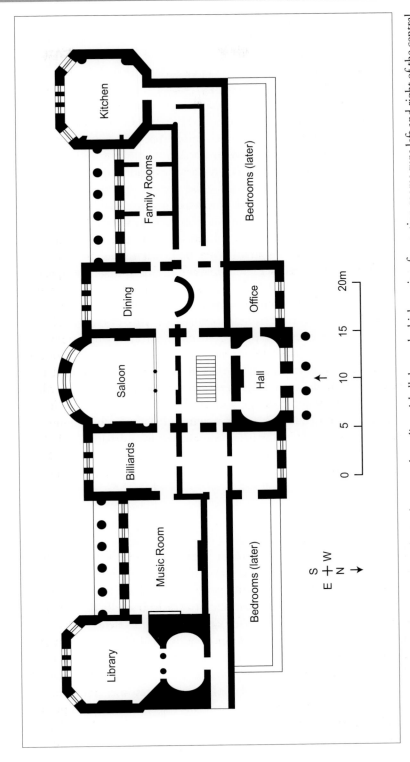

5.26. Heaton Hall: another new-style plan with a central top-lit stairhall, beyond which a suite of reception rooms runs left and right of the central saloon. (This plan is drawn to a smaller scale than the others, but the main block is about as wide as Lytham Hall.)

becoming accessible to West Europeans). These discoveries surprised the men who made them and wrote about them (since they were used to seeing Roman architecture through Palladio's eyes) and they fascinated many of those who read their books. They showed that the room shapes of some Roman buildings had been more varied than Burlington and his friends had believed. They also revealed that Roman buildings had been decorated in ways known to, but discarded by, Palladio.

All this led before long to the realisation that Palladian 'correctness' was a mistake – made in good faith, no doubt, but without a basis in reality. With each year that passed, research extended the repertoire of genuinely Roman decorative motifs. The conclusion was soon drawn that, if there was no single ideal of perfection, sanctioned by Roman examples, then patrons and designers were free to choose what motifs they liked – within the Classical tradition, of course, or, as they said, in the 'antique manner'; or even to make slight variations on traditional themes. Why should people be hidebound, they asked, by a now discredited canon of taste? Palladian design, which had been accepted as authoritative, was coming to be regarded as a sort of aberration.

At much the same time some antiquarians also began to discover buildings in Greece (still part of the Ottoman empire), and similar ones in southern Italy, and also statues and vases which had been made by Greeks. These were obviously older than Roman buildings and artefacts, and some people therefore considered them to be more authentically Classical. These Greek buildings also used decorative motifs – stylised honeysuckle flowers, a Doric column without a base, and a flat-faced Ionic capital – which had not been known before and which were soon added to the Classical repertoire and used with some enthusiasm. The general view was, however, that the later Romans had merely refined Greek ideas and therefore still provided better models for contemporary designers.

Another consequence was that a few serious-minded young men doing the Grand Tour in Italy also began a life-long interest in the art of the Greco-Roman world. The Tour was meant to be a sort of cultural pilgrimage-cum-finishing school for young gentlemen, but most merely lived *la dolce vita* with their friends and brought back some souvenirs. For a few, however, like two (Catholic) Lancastrians, Charles Towneley and Henry Blundell (who knew each other and met in Rome in 1776–7), the Tour prompted a fervent ambition to build up collections of genuine 'antique' statuary, which we can still see today. Blundell had a pair of temples built around 1800 at Ince Blundell to house his collection – one in the shape and with the name of the Pantheon in Rome. [It can be seen on the right in illustration 5.7.] Most of the Classical pieces which formed his collection are now in the Liverpool Museum. Towneley had thought of something similar and in 1788 had asked the Italian architect,

5.27. Towneley Hall: Zoffany's portrait of Charles Towneley (sitting on the right), with some friends and his collection of Classical antiques. The picture cannot be factually correct, since the floor would probably have buckled under the weight of the statues.

Joseph Bonomi, to design a Rotunda in Towneley Hall; but nothing was built, and his collection stayed in his London house. It had been portrayed there in 1781 with him and some friends in a conversation piece painted by Johann Zoffany, which is now at Towneley Hall [5.27]. His collection, known as the 'Towneley Marbles', was bought for the British Museum in 1805 and can be seen there today. [9]

The finest examples of antique-manner (or, as we would say, Neo-Classical) decoration in Lancashire are at **Heaton Hall**, whose plan has already been shown [5.25]. The three main rooms have ceilings decorated with exquisitely elegant low-relief plasterwork by the younger Joseph Rose of York, using newly fashionable motifs, like fluted fans, garlands of wheat-ears and stylized honeysuckle flowers, standing out in white against the pinks, greens and blues which were also in fashion. Over each of the fireplaces in the saloon (which no longer have integral chimneypieces) is an oval plaque with a bas-relief of a muse, framed within a garland of wheat-ears and flanked by a pair of alcoves containing copies of antique statues [5.28]. The dining room has, opposite its Venetian window, a shallow round-headed apsidal alcove, containing the side tables designed by Wyatt to carry a display of family silver. The ceilings of the room and the alcove are decorated with paintings by the Italian artist, Biaggio Rebecca, done in oils and then pasted up; they represent the four seasons and (in the niche) three dancing priestesses of Bacchus. [5.29]

There is a similar alcove, but with a segmental head, in the dining room at **Lytham** which, with the drawing room, was remodelled in the antique manner in 1797 [5.30]. The side table within the alcove was made by Gillow's of Lancaster at the same time. [10] This delicate plasterwork, used sparingly in the pilasters around the room, is the last produced for use on walls in a Lancashire gentry house, though plaster decoration on ceilings continued throughout the nineteenth century. Thereafter walls were decorated, if at all, by fixed paintings, as in the billiards room at Heaton, or by wallpapers – printed, until the 1830s, by hand from carved blocks. At first these imitated the textile hangings, fashionable earlier in the century in aristocratic houses. There are, I think, no examples on the walls of Lancashire houses, but at **Temple Newsam**, near **Leeds**, some originals and some modern reprints from old blocks can be seen. The Whitworth Art Gallery in Manchester has, in its reserve, the largest collection of wallpapers outside the Victoria and Albert Museum.

The stairhall at **Heaton Hall** is rather austere and leads only to family rooms, but is the grandest space in the house; its staircase is of the imperial pattern, and its fine wrought-iron balustrade continues around the corridor at its head. The lampstandards are based on a tripod found at Herculaneum. The main room on the first floor, the so-called Cupola Room above the saloon, was the circular drawing room of an apartment for Egerton's widowed mother [5.31]. There are a few antique-manner plaques, but the main decorative motifs are arch-headed recesses, framed between pairs

5.28. Heaton Hall: the saloon with its exquisite antique manner plasterwork on walls and ceiling.

5.29. Heaton Hall: the alcove in the dining room, decorated with paintings of priestess of Bacchus.

of plasterwork pilasters. These pilasters were exquisitely painted by Rebecca, with what are called 'grotesques' – delicate drops of scrollwork, small medallions, vases and griffons. The domed ceiling, which gives the room its name, is similarly decorated. Such motifs had been discovered during the excavation of Roman buildings around 1500, then briefly used in Renaissance Italy – in Raphael's Vatican Loggia in Rome, for example – but then dropped for some reason from the repertoire. They were introduced to England by Burlington's protégé, William Kent, at Kensington Palace in the 1720s and then popularised by Adam in the 1760s, along with other antique-manner motifs. They are called grotesques, not because they are mis-shapen, but because they were discovered in rooms which were below the contemporary ground-level in Rome and therefore called by the Italians *grotte* [= caves]. In the drawing room at **Lytham Hall** there are examples of similar work, provided by Gillow's in 1797; they are not so fine

5.30. Lytham Hall: antique manner plasterwork in the dining room.

– or have been badly restored – but they are interesting because they also include rural scenes.

Heaton Hall contains the finest collection of eighteenth-century furniture in Lancashire. Most pieces have been brought from elsewhere by Manchester City Council, which owns the building, but a few are original to the house – like the Wyatt tables in the apse of the dining room and the Gillow bookcases in the library. Lewis Wyatt, a nephew of James Wyatt, remodelled the library at Heaton in 1823 within his uncle's octagonal shell [5.32]. He used Greek motifs – notably the flat-faced Ionic capitals of the screen. They were fashionable in the 1820s and '30s, and appropriate for a library, because they had overtones of culture and scholarship; but they soon fell from favour.

A library was the second of the specialised rooms introduced into Georgian houses. Over two centuries it had developed from a collection of books in an owner's private closet, to a book-lined study (of which there is a good example of around 1730 at **Dunham Massey**, near Altrincham). Then it became, as at Heaton, a larger and communal room where an owner could display his leather-bound volumes and thus his knowledge and culture, and also where guests could read books or write letters, and where men could find peace and quiet during the day. (Women tended to use the boudoir of the lady of the house for this purpose.) The finest library in the North West is at **Tatton Park**, near Knutsford, which was designed around 1810 by Lewis Wyatt. Its fitted bookcases and furniture are by Gillow's.

The entrance front of Heaton Hall is very plain – basically that of Egerton's father's house, but with only two storeys plus a Tuscan portico; the seven-bay wings to either side, which contained bedrooms, may not have been completed until 1823. In contrast, the south-facing garden front has always been an impressive show façade [5.33]. Its centre is about as wide as Lytham Hall, but it is lower and then is considerably extended into two pavilions – much as at Platt Hall but more elegantly. The house makes its impact in the landscape by width

5.31. Heaton Hall: the fireplace in the Cupola Room, showing also grotesques painted on the pilasters.

rather than height, and gives the impression that it is much larger than it really is – almost a house of parade rather than a villa-plus. It also provides a good and attractive example of the 'movement', about which Adam often wrote but which he seldom achieved – that is, the contrast of geometric forms, the change of height between them, and the play of recession and projection and of light and shadow. The façade is, of course, symmetrical. The two-storey central block has neither pediment nor portico, but a bow, decorated with giant Ionic colimns, and a low dome – attractive ideas which were probably derived from an unbuilt plan for Kedleston. On either side is a Venetian window (lighting the dining room on the left and the billiards room on the right) and then a low, five-bay colonnade, which presents some contrast of light and shade, and finally a taller octagonal block (with another Venetian window); the one on the left accommodates the kitchen, and the other one the library – rooms of very different character but similarly clad.

.32. Heaton Hall:
Greek – that is, flat-
aced – Ionic capitals
n the library.

33. Heaton Hall: the garden façade – Wyatt's version of Adam's 'movement' hides the fact that the
brary is in the nearer octagonal pavilion, with the kitchen in the further one. This photograph was
ken, by chance, on a day when the Hall was closed to the public. It shows the house as it will have
ppeared for much of the year when the family was away – with the shutters closed.

The house stands within an extensive park, designed by William Emes, a pupil of 'Capability' Brown; work was – sensibly – begun before the house was started. A few of the rooms have French windows, to give easy access to the garden, whose lawns, within the ha-ha, sweep up almost to the house, as fashion was then dictating. [11] Little remains now of the original planting scheme at Heaton, but the park still contains the contemporary Stables, and its approach roads pass two fine gatehouses.

References

[1]   W. John and K. Smith, *An Architectural History of Towneley Hall, Burnley* (2004), p. 50.

[2]   The plans are in John Woolfe and James Gandon, *Vitruvius Britannicus*, volume 4 (1767) plates 94–98.

[3]   J. J. Bagley, *A History of Lancashire* (1976), p. 94.

[4]   Both Carr's and Lightoler's façades are illustrated in Clare Hartwell and Nikolaus Pevsner, *Lancashire: Manchester and the South East* (2004), p. 473.

[5]   Matthew Hyde and Nikolaus Pevsner, *The Buildings of England: Cumbria* (2010), p. 347.

[6]   John Champness, *Thomas Harrison, Georgian Architect of Chester and Lancaster* (2005), pp. 29–30.

[7]   Mark Girouard, *Life in the English Country House* (1978), pp.194–8.

[8]   Ruth Shrigley (*pers. comm.*).

[9]   Jacqueline Riding, 'At home with the Connoisseurs' in *Art Quarterly* (Summer 2007), pp. 28–31.

[10]   Susan Stuart (*pers. comm.*).

[11]   An attractive example of this more relaxed treatment of gardens is in one of the famous 'Red Books' which the landscape architect, Humphrey Repton, produced in 1793 for Lathom House; it has lawns replacing a formal water feature in front of the house. This can be seen in the Lancashire Record Office (where a CD is obtainable), and two drawings from it are illustrated in *The Art Fund's 2004 Review*, p. 101.

o. Blackwell, with its lakeland setting evident in the distance, as it appeared for much of the year when
e family was away – with the shutters closed.

6.1. Scarisbrick Hall: a picture in the chimneypiece of the Red Drawing Room, showing the house as designed by Augustus Pugin.

CHAPTER SIX

Gentry Houses in the Nineteenth Century

Introduction

Nineteenth-century England arguably came to an abrupt and bloody end in the autumn of 1914, as two rows of defensive trenches zig-zagged their way across northern France towards the Channel coast. Its beginning was less clear, but it too was related to war. A few houses had been built during the wars against France between 1793 and 1815, but the rise in the number of building projects in the years after 1815 is noticeable. It must relate to such factors as easier access to Baltic timber and loans at lower rates of interest, which were the result of peace; another factor was the fortunes made during the war itself. However, the coming of peace did not alter attitudes to housing, and the changes of plan and accommodation – of Commodity – which had been introduced in the middle of the eighteenth century, continued with few modifications. Reception rooms had returned to the ground floor – nearly always above low and almost invisible cellars – and stayed there. Dining rooms and libraries and the asymmetrical plans, which allowed easy access to all rooms, were normal until the end of the nineteenth century and beyond.

However, in the matter of Delight, individual house builders and their architects felt more free to choose the decorative motifs which pleased them most. At first, these were mainly from the Classical repertoire, but after about 1830 the style in which a house was decorated became less a matter of social convention and more a result of the conscious choice of the owner. The story of gentry house building in the nineteenth century is therefore largely concerned with an overlapping succession of decorative styles; a chosen style was a statement about an owner's self-perception. However, as the century wore on, more and more houses were designed in approximate imitation of traditional English houses, as though to stress – or suggest – the long gentry pedigree of their builders.

Builders

There were significant changes among the builders of gentry houses in Lancashire during the nineteenth century, which once more set it a little apart from many English counties. The growth in the wealth and therefore of the economic power of the industrial and commercial middle classes, already mentioned, led slowly towards the ultimately terminal decline of the political power of the gentry – but not of their social influence. A number of large houses were built or rebuilt by old families during the first half of the century, but by the 1850s most such families felt themselves to be well-enough housed. Furthermore, in the second half of the century a number of them moved away from Lancashire, especially from the industrial areas where their social status was questioned and the amenity of their estates was diminished.

With few exceptions, therefore, the largest new houses in the second half of the century were built by newly-rich families. Much the same was also true in other counties near the growing industrial conurbations. More often than not, though, these houses stood in no more than large, park-like gardens, and were maintained from the profits of the families' trade or industry. Rather like Bushell's house at Goosnargh or Bank Hall on the outskirts of Warrington in the eighteenth century, they were largish suburban houses in the countryside, and not gentry houses proper in the middle of an agricultural estate. There are a couple near every industrial town, often now in a public park: Stubbylee Hall at Bacup [6.2] is an early example, with Greaves Park at Lancaster from the middle of the century and what is now the Haworth Art Gallery at Accrington from the very end of the period.

6.2. Stubbylee Hall: a villa with Greek decorative details for a local factory owner

Newly wealthy men sometimes bought whole estates in attractive areas. In 1799 the Blackburn cotton-manufacturer, Henry Sudell, built Woodfold Hall to a fine classical design in the middle of an extensive park near Mellor. The example of Thomas Miller at Singleton has already been quoted in chapter four. In 1857 William Preston, a merchant and former mayor of Liverpool, bought the Ellel Grange estate and rebuilt the house, now a <u>private</u> college. Its two Italianate towers – following the model of Queen Victoria's Osborne House – can be glimpsed from the canal towpath south of Galgate. Somewhat similarly John Wilson-Patten, who had sold Bank Hall to Warrington Borough Council in 1870, rebuilt Winmarleigh Hall (a <u>private</u> house) in a vaguely Elizabethan manner and lived there as a country gentleman: his family had long owned the estate. When he was offered a peerage in 1874, he took the title of Lord Winmarleigh. A few years later it was the turn of James Williamson, the 'linoleum king of Lancaster'. He had lived at Ryelands House in Skerton since 1874, making significant extensions there; when the opportunity arose, he bought Ashton Hall as his country seat in 1884. He accepted a peerage in 1895 and chose the title of Lord Ashton.

Commodity

The housing needs of gentry families remained largely unchanged throughout the nineteenth century, and the basic form of their houses reflected this. Every house had a double-pile plan and that trinity of reception rooms, inherited from the previous century – a library, a dining room and a drawing room, normally laid out *en suite*. Some drawing rooms were particularly large to facilitate major entertaining. Bedrooms were always upstairs, so that staircases were only used by the family and their guests. Nevertheless, stairhalls, which were often linked with the entrance hall, were always impressively high and spacious, containing an open-well or an imperial staircase.

Some new rooms were introduced in the course of the nineteenth century, as changing fashions demanded. The most striking one was a billiards room, often top-lit and at first for men only. One was built at **Leighton Hall** in the 1820s on the ground floor, when the house was remodelled. It is now used as the dining room, but the skylight is still visible. At **Holker** a billiards room was included in the new suite of ground-floor rooms built in the West Wing after a fire in 1871, but at **Lytham Hall** the billiards room was added above a service room in the 1880s, and at **Levens Hall** in the 1890s above the hall. At the end of the century women played too, and in new houses tables were often placed in the large entrance hall, sometimes with a raised dais or first-floor balcony from which family and friends could watch the game – as at **Broadleys** or what is now the **Haworth Art Gallery** in **Accrington**.

This was part of the process – well seen in the West Wing at **Holker** – whereby relatively more space was given to communal areas like libraries and drawing rooms than to private bedrooms and dressing rooms. Once hot-water heating systems were common, houses could be extended into conservatories or winter gardens. (The thirteenth Earl of Derby even had hot-water central heating installed in his aviary at Knowsley in the 1830s.) Most early conservatories have since disappeared, but there is an orangery, dating from 1823, at **Heaton Hall** and an attractive conservatory (of 1826) with a cast-iron structure in the (occasionally open) garden at **Dallam Tower** [6.3]. The conservatory at **Leighton Hall** was recently rebuilt to the original design of 1870.

A particular feature of Victorian houses was the growth in the size and complexity of service wings, which were kept away to one side or at the back. At **Scarisbrick Hall** the service wing stretches back at right-angles to the main façade as far as the main façade is wide. Thurland Castle offers a fascinating example with its accommodation on three different levels, reflecting the social status of the people involved – with the family house above the kitchen and laundry, which stand above the stables and garden sheds. Each level had (and still has) a different access from the main gate. The park and house are not open to the public, but the three paths can just be made out on the OS Pathfinder map and can be seen in a recently published aerial photograph.[1]

Household servants were kept virtually invisible. Near Cuerden Hall, at the point where a path from Bamber Bridge to the service wing crossed the drive to the house, the servants had to use a tunnel. In the houses themselves they were summoned by bells from the servants' hall. Families thought that this was mutually advantageous, and in 1864 the architect, Robert Kerr, wrote:

6.3. Dallam Tower: the cast-iron conservatory of 1826.

'The family constitute one community, the servants another. Whatever may be their mutual regard as dwellers under one roof, each class is entitled to shut its doors upon the other and be alone…What passes on either side of the boundary shall be invisible and inaudible on the other…On both sides privacy is highly valued.'[2]

The views of servants – who were strictly disciplined by the butler and housekeeper – are, however, only rarely on the record.[3] In fact many Victorian masters did try hard to exert some control over the behaviour of their staff. The bedrooms of men servants were kept rigidly separate from those of women servants. Daily prayers, at which attendance was compulsory for indoor staff at least, were common, and chapels were built in several houses; one, dating from 1855, is clearly visible from the A588 to the right at **Thurnham Hall** [6.4], which is now a private country club. It is fair to add that most household servants probably had better accommodation and food than their relatives outside.

Delight

By 1800 many reference books were available, and any architect worth his salt could design in any style to meet the personal tastes of his clients. It was at first, basically, a question of dressing up the symmetrical Georgian box, using motifs associated with this or that style to decorate a room or a whole building. Thomas Hopper wrote in 1837 that 'it is an architect's business to understand all styles and to be prejudiced in favour of none',[4] and he practised what he preached. However, in Lancashire at least, much of the significant work before the middle of the century was done

.4. Thurnham
Hall: social control of
ervants in 1855, by
means of a chapel
uilt next to the re-
onted Elizabethan
ouse.

in a Classical idiom, which had associations with the education given to most gentlemen and had overtones of dignity and self-respect.

Classical

Most of this work was designed for old-established families in existing houses, as at Browsholme in 1805 and at Towneley after 1814. In both cases the architect was a nephew of James Wyatt – Jeffrey Wyatt, who was later known as Sir Jeffrey Wyattville. At **Browsholme** he remodelled the drawing room [6.5] in a graceful manner with a flat ceiling, framed by fashionable segmental arches along each wall and in the corners carried on broad pilasters with shallow round-headed niches. He decorated the heads of the doorcases, however, with little cartouches of vaguely Elizabethan motifs – perhaps to recall the origins of the house and please his client, Thomas Lister Parker, whose varied antiquarian interests are still displayed in the entrance hall. At **Towneley** he designed two fine high rooms on the ground floor of the south wing (the medieval tower) for Peregrine Towneley – the dining room, which has a ceiling with segmental arches similar to those at Browsholme, and the grander drawing room [6.6], which has a shallow coved ceiling. On the outside of the building, however, Wyatt nodded again to the past by refashioning the windows of these reception rooms with round heads and square hoodmoulds, and by giving mullions back to most other windows. He also linked the dining room to the kitchen in the north wing by means of a half-hidden tunnel outside the house, running underneath the

6.5. Browsholme Hall: J. C. Buckler's drawing, dated 1814, of the recently designed Drawing Room.

6. Towneley Hall: the classical Drawing Room of *c*.1815. The elegant fireplace dates from *c*.1770.

castellated hall porch (which he had added) so that servants could carry food to and from the dining room without having to pass through the hall, which was by then an integral part of the family's house.

The biggest Classical house of the period was **Haigh Hall**, now the centre-piece of a country park. It has some fine interiors, including a spacious, domed staircase hall with an impressive imperial staircase, but it is seldom open to the public. The house was designed by its owner, the twenty-fourth Earl of Crawford and Balcarres, who was a talented engineer. His father had inherited the estate in 1787 after marrying the Bradshaigh heiress. The house was built in stages between 1827 and 1840 to replace the old Haigh Hall, which had been damaged by mining subsidence; it was in effect a new house. The old house had been modelled on Gawthorpe Hall, and this is reflected in the three full-height bay-windows on the new hall's garden façade [6.7]. The two-and-a-half- storey, eleven-bay entrance façade – the last part to be rebuilt – is imposing in its dignified restraint, with a Tuscan portico set between a pair of two-bay projections, whose vertical emphasis neatly offsets the façade's width.

One of the best, and most accessible, of the gentry houses built in a Classical style is the handsome **Shaw Hill** at **Whittle-le-Woods**, which is now a hotel, golf and country club [6.8]. It was built in 1807, on an old site with a wide view to the west, for Thomas Crosse, whose family had lived there for some generations. In 1846 it was substantially remodelled by the Birkenhead architect, Charles Reed, for a Liverpool merchant, Thomas Bright Ikin, who had married the Crosse heiress in 1828 and taken her surname, like John Carrill-Worsley at Platt. As Thomas Bright Crosse, he was made High Sheriff in 1837, which marked his acceptance into County society.

6.7. Haigh Hall: a lithograph of 1847, showing the recently rebuilt house.

6.8. Shaw Hill: a lithograph of 1847, showing the original house of 1807 and it lower service wing to the left; the entrance façade was re-modelled in 1846 with a full-width portico.

The general form of the house, whose main façades have five bays and two and a half storeys, with a prominent bow-window on the garden front, must date from 1807; so too must the spacious open-well staircase, which has an elegant wrought-iron balustrade, decorated with the Crosse family's emblem of a stork. The upper part of the stairhall, however, with its round-headed arches carried on heavy pilastered piers, and the more richly decorated window surrounds and the full-width Doric portico on the entrance façade must be part of Reed's work. Shaw Hill was probably the last Classical house to be built in Lancashire for an old-established gentry family – albeit partly with new money; it is a not unworthy example.

Gothick

The first work done outside the Classical tradition was carried out in the 1820s and 1830s in what people then called the 'Gothick'. This style, using decorative motifs from the Middle Ages, had been used occasionally in the eighteenth century in new work in an old context, where a classically based design was felt to be inappropriate. The first example of this in Lancashire is the plain and battlemented **Museum** at **Clitheroe Castle**, which was built as the steward's house in 1743, apparently to the designs of the Castle's owner, the second Duke of Montagu. Finer examples are the tower of Lancaster Priory Church, designed by Henry Sephton in the 1750s, and Thomas Harrison's County Gaol and Shire Hall at Lancaster, which date from the 1790s.[5]

Another attractive example of this sensitive designing in the context of an old house is **Broughton Tower** at Broughton-in-Furness [6.9]. (It is now <u>private</u> flats, but visible from the drive.) In 1744 a member of the Gilpin Sawrey family had built a five-bay house in front of a medieval tower, and in 1777 this was refaced with Gothick details – perhaps to stress the house's medieval origins. The architect, possibly John Hird of Cartmel, gave all the windows ogee heads and placed a pretty ogee-headed porch, framed by clustered columns, in front of the main entrance. In 1882–3 the house was courteously, but – on purpose, not quite symmetrically – extended by the addition of a tower to right and left.

6.9. Broughton Tower: the Gothick façade of 1777 in front of the medieval tower; the outer towers date from 1882–3.

The wars against France, which began in 1793, cut England off from the Continent, thereby helping to encourage an interest in English landscapes and buildings. By the early 1800s George III came to regard the Gothick style as a sort of bulwark against the French, symbolic of the Magna Carta rather than the Rights of Man.[6] To encourage patriotism he employed James Wyatt to Gothicise parts of Windsor Castle. (Much of this work was, however, sumptuously rebuilt at enormous expense after 1824 for George IV to the designs of Sir Jeffrey Wyattville, who basically produced the Windsor Castle which visitors see today.) The king's example was, of course, widely followed.

The finest Gothick house in Lancashire is **Conishead Priory,** which now belongs to a Buddhist community who are restoring it carefully [6.10]. It was begun in 1823 to the designs of Philip Wyatt, a son of James, for Colonel Thomas Bradyll. A turnpike road had recently been laid out past Bradyll's old house, Samlesbury Hall, near Preston, so he decided to build a new seat on one of the family's other properties, where an Elizabethan house, rather like Gawthorpe, stood on the site of an old monastery. Most of the rather rambling building of rendered brickwork was, however, designed by the Kendal architect, George Webster, after 1838. It is arranged asymmetrically around a tall entrance block, dominated by a four-light Gothic window and two octagonal turrets – doubtless to recall the monastic origins of the site. The front door leads to the church-like entrance hall, which rises two storeys beneath a vaulted ceiling and is lit by stained glass windows. Beyond the hall an attractive long corridor, also vaulted, runs like an internal cloister to left and right, linking most of the main rooms. To the left the impressively spacious

6.10. Conishead Priory: a photograph of c. 1880, showing the asymmetrical façade of the Gothick house – with reception rooms to the left and some service rooms to the right.

.11. Leighton Hall:
ie Gothick front of
ie early 1820s, with
ie tower of 1870 to
ie left, making the
ouse fashionably
symmetrical.

stairhall, again lit by stained glass windows, contains a wide imperial staircase, at the top of which another corridor acts as a gallery giving a striking view of the entrance hall. One of the upper rooms contains seventeenth-century panelling, brought from Samlesbury.

Less impressive, but more immediately attractive is **Leighton Hall** [6.11], which is built of a very white limestone and sits in a half-saucer of tree-framed pasture, backed by the Lake District hills. What visitors see now is a Gothick re-facing of a simple medium-sized Georgian house, built c.1760, which had two storeys above cellars. It is illustrated on the back cover of this book and must have looked like a smaller version of Platt Hall. This remodelling was done for Richard Gillow in the early 1820s – perhaps by the Preston architect, Robert Roper, who was responsible for the Gothick refronting of the Dalton family's basically Elizabethan house, Thurnham Hall [6.4].

This Richard Gillow was a son of Richard Gillow, the Georgian furniture designer and architect (who had perhaps designed the earlier house). He had continued to manage the family business but had recently bought the Leighton estate from a cousin. His wife was related to the Stapletons of Carleton Hall, the major Catholic gentry family in East Yorkshire, and she must have been delighted, when her husband was able to sell the business and retire to live the life of a country gentleman in a house full of fine, fashionable Gillow furniture. There is a portrait of him in the hall, and his pose suggests that he too was not displeased by his change of lifestyle.

Much of the Gothick work at Leighton is no more than skin-deep, and Georgian details can be glimpsed in doors and cornices on the first floor and, outside, around the corner, in the stableyard – places which contemporary visitors would not have seen. The entrance hall, however, which is the most beautiful room in the house [6.12], has a structural cast-iron screen of three shallow arches on clustered columns separating it from the stair-hall, where the cantilever staircase sweeps gently upwards in front of a traceried window. The stone treads of the staircase probably predate the Gothick work, but their balusters are miniature versions of the columns of the screen.

Tudorbethan

The pointed windows and medieval overtones of design in the Gothick idiom did not appeal to everybody, and from the 1830s a number of houses were built in a manner which, while having associations with the Good Old Days, was somewhat more convenient. It is often now called the Tudorbethan style. The best Lancashire example is **Whittington Hall**, a <u>private</u> house, which can be glimpsed from the B6254 [6.13]. Here an older house was rebuilt on a larger scale in the early 1830s for Thomas Greene by George Webster. Greene came from an old family of lawyers, who had lived for generations at Slyne, which was by then on a busy turnpike. He was also the Tory MP for Lancaster and had recently married the daughter of a baronet; wanting a more suitable home, he bought the Whittington estate. His new house has a symmetrical seven-bay façade with four gabled dormers and two two-storey bay-windows in the wide cross-wings. All the main windows have mullions and transoms.

6.12. Leighton Hall: the entrance hall with the elegant cast-iron screen dividing it from the stair-hall. The portrait of Richard Gillow is on the left.

6.13. Whittington
Hall: a lithograph of
1847, showing the
recently built
Tudorbethan house,
and its tower.

Behind the façade there is a battlemented tower; it may stand on
medieval foundations, or it may merely be there to suggest that the new
house occupies a medieval site.[7]

A number of other gentry houses were built in this Tudorbethan
manner, and they are among the most attractive houses in the county. A
fine example is **Capernwray Hall,** now a <u>private</u> college, but visible from
a public road [6.14]. It was begun in 1844 by the Lancaster architect,
Edmund Sharpe, to remodel and extend a fairly recent house on the site,
and was completed in 1848 by Graham Paley, Sharpe's new partner and
later successor. Their client was George Marton, whose family had owned
the estate for a century. The house is almost symmetrical on both the
entrance front and the garden façade around the corner, and composes
picturesquely from the original drive. The garden façade has two fine,

6.14. Capernwray
Hall: a photograph of
c.1880 showing the
entrance façade, and
tower.

two-storey square bay-windows with panels of tracery, lighting the former dining room and drawing room and the bedrooms above. From the two-storey porch on the entrance front a sort of cross-passage leads to the impressive top-lit stairhall, which rises – as at Conishead – the whole height of the house and contains an open-well staircase. The tower, which rises above the large service court behind the house, is not medieval but, as at Whittington, suggests that the site is an old one.

Gothic Revival

Gothick and Tudorbethan were little more than the cosmetic application of medieval motifs to Georgian houses. Most of us probably find them pleasing enough, but to Augustus Pugin, the man who (in Mark Girouard's memorable words) 'transformed the Gothic Revival from a fashion to a crusade',[8] they were utterly abhorrent. Pugin was the son of a French émigré draughtsman, who had trained him so well – by encouraging him to sketch medieval remains in England and France – that, after his father died in 1832, it was recognised that, although he was only twenty, he knew more about the appearance of medieval art and architecture than anyone in England.

6.15. Scarisbrick Hall: Augutus Pugin's hall dominates the façade as it might have done in the Middle Ages.

He was therefore asked by Charles Barry to help with the decorative details for his entry in the competition for the new Houses of Parliament, and when this scheme won in 1836, Pugin's name was made. In the previous year he had converted to Catholicism, and this served to strengthen his highly idealised view of the Middle Ages and his architectural convictions.

Pugin believed that the interior plan of a building should determine its outward appearance, as it had done in medieval times. (An architect nowadays would say that form should follow function.) In consequence, a symmetrical façade, like the garden front at Heaton, was deceitful and even immoral. Furthermore he could not accept Hopper's view that an architect should be able to design in any style and believed that Gothic was the only appropriate style for a Christian English gentlemen to use for his house.

He was in many ways the Victorian equivalent of the Georgian Lord Burlington, equally serious but much more passionate. In his own work he aimed to use medieval motifs, accurately drawn from real examples, in such a way as would allow him not just to produce an archaeologically-correct decorative overlay, but also to revive an authentic Gothic architecture in Victorian England. In 1837 this uncompromising attitude brought him to the attention of the Catholic squire, Charles Scarisbrick, who wanted to continue the remodelling of his ancestral home near Southport, which dated from around 1595.

When Pugin received this commission, **Scarisbrick Hall** – now a <u>private</u> school, but occasionally open to the public – was a recently built, double-pile Gothick house, fairly symmetrical around a two-storey hall, which had been created by the removal of the floor of the room above it, the Elizabethan great chamber. Pugin's aim was to remodel and embellish this hall to make it look authentically medieval, as though it was the unchanged heart of the ancestral home of an old-established family [6.15]. As Rufford Old Hall shows, the hall of a medieval house was the dominant feature of its exterior, and Pugin made it so at Scarisbrick. Inside too, it is the tallest, most spacious and most splendid room in the house, rising to an ornate and painted timber roof [6.16]. As in medieval times, it is the first room seen by visitors and is entered, at the 'lower' end, through the equivalent of a cross-passage.

The hall is also interesting, because it is the only surviving example in Lancashire of what was a short-lived fashion for 'baronial' halls. These were built by a few early Victorian landowners, who were frightened by the upsurge of radical political movements like Chartism, which brought

6.16. Scarisbrick Hall: the interior of the 'baronial hall' with its high open roof and 'cross passage' in the background.

to mind memories of bloody revolutions in France in 1789, and 1830. They countered these fears with the ideals of the 'One Nation Toryism', preached by the young Benjamin Disraeli (then a novelist rather than a politician) and others. These men aimed to revive the medieval ideal of 'good lordship' by stressing the duties as well as the privileges of gentry status and wealth, and by encouraging owners to treat their tenants well – with what they called 'old English hospitality'. This may have been little more than a symbolic and self-interested gesture on their part, but Charles Scarisbrick did in fact enjoy the reputation of being a good landlord.

Another such hall is at the astonishingly authentic-looking **Peckforton Castle** in Cheshire, which was built between 1844 and 1851 to the designs of Anthony Salvin. Its owner, the first Lord Tollemache, was also true to his Tory paternalism: he gave to each of the labourers on his enormous estate a decent cottage and three acres – which cost him four times what he spent on his new house. Furthermore, he wrote that that 'the only real and lasting pleasure to be derived from the possession of a landed estate is to witness the improvement in the social conditions of those residing in it'.[9]

The most beautiful of Pugin's rooms at Scarisbrick Hall, though it is rather dark, is the Kings' Room. It is named after the twenty-seven portraits of English and Scottish kings and queens from Henry VII to James I, probably copied by Edmund Parris from paintings in the royal collection but probably not at Pugin's suggestion.[10] [Part of it is pictured on the back cover.] Its combination of rich but disciplined decoration – the portraits are framed by colonnettes and canopies under the vaulted cove of the ceiling – recalls, on a small scale, the Houses of Parliament.

Parris also produced another interesting painting for the chimneypiece in what is now called the Red Drawing Room, although it was built as a library [6.1]. It is a work of Romantic nostalgia, showing Charles Scarisbrick and his family in 'medieval' dress in front of Scarisbrick Hall, as it had been designed for him by Pugin – with the hall, its bay-windows and porch placed between the two projecting cross-wings and the tower. However, the tower and right-hand wing are lower and less ornate than the present ones. This is because when Charles died in 1860 without legitimate heirs, his elder sister, Anne, inherited the property. There had been little love lost between them, and Anne, who was by now the wealthy widow of a Derbyshire baronet, felt that she could afford to place her mark on the east wing of what was now her house. She chose as her architect Augustus Pugin's son, Edward, who had done some work at the Hall since his father's death in 1852. Before looking at this work, however, it is appropriate to look first at a couple of other houses.

*   *   *

Augustus Pugin was a fanatic who worked himself to death by the age of 40. He failed to achieve a significant following among architects, but he did have some influence. When in 1853, for example, William Le Gendre Starkie, a member of the family at Huntroyde, bought the estate containing **Ashton Hall** – private, but visible from the A588 – he decided to replace the hall, which dated from Jacobean times, with something more 'medieval' [6.17]. And he had some success: to the right of the genuinely medieval tower, he designed – perhaps with the help of

6.17. Ashton Hall: the hall and tower of 1856 balancing the genuine medieval tower on the left.

Graham Paley – a tall, open hall with a bay-window and then a two-storey tower with turrets at the corners, which balances the older one. The porch leads to a cross-passage and then, on the left, to the hall which has a slightly spindly hammer-beam roof.

Paley also designed **Wennington Hall** for William Saunders in 1855. It is now a <u>private</u> school, but is visible from the road to Melling [6.18]. It replaced an older house, which Saunders' father, a Liverpool merchant, had bought with its estate in 1841. Thanks to the influence of Pugin, the six-bay, two-storey façade is no longer symmetrical, though it is balanced. The three-storey porch with its pointed door stands on the left against a

6.18. Wennington Hall: a balanced but not symmetrical façade, plus tower.

three-storey cross-wing, while to the right is a two-storey cross-wing with a bay-window on both floors. All the windows have mullions and transoms, and a few have pointed tops. The site is old, but the two towers are not.

Such towers are quite common in North Lancashire, where the genuinely medieval and highly visible tower at **Hornby Castle** must have provided the model for people to emulate.[10] The first example was probably the entrance tower built around 1805 in front of a medieval tower at **Gresgarth Hall** near Caton. (The house is private, but the exterior is visible from the beautiful gardens which are occasionally open.) The last of these 'medieval' towers is at **Leighton Hall** and was added by Paley and his new partner, Hubert Austin, in 1870. It provided the welcome associations of a long-standing gentry pedigree and also created a fashionably picturesque façade of controlled asymmetry, with height and bulk played off against length [6.11].

*   *   *

Edward Pugin, although his ideas were different from his father's, must have felt challenged to emulate his father's work. His generation recognised that medieval 'authenticity' was impossible to achieve and adopted a more relaxed attitude to the past. They made no attempt to create buildings which might look as though they had been built in the Middle Ages; instead they chose to use medieval motifs which they and their clients liked for their appearance and associations – a picturesque rather than a pedantic approach. His work for Lady Anne Scarisbrick at **Scarisbrick Hall** in the 1860s is the best Lancashire example of this more eclectic Gothic Revival design.

He added a very long service wing, modern conveniences like gas lighting and central heating, and commissioned the attractive medieval-looking stained-glass windows representing the Christian Virtues, the Seasons and the Arts and Sciences in Lady Anne's bedroom and drawing room. (The windows were made by Hardman's of Birmingham.) But the exterior of the east wing is where he made the greatest impact on the older building [6.19]. He gave the wing a greater vertical emphasis, with long windows rising into richly gabled dormers. Above all, in every sense of the term, he replaced the tower which his father had designed (and which had been the model for the 'Big Ben' clock tower at Westminster) with a taller one, with long windows, pinnacles and a spire to emphasise its height. This he calculated to a nicety, so that it should dominate the ensemble without dwarfing his father's work. Lady Anne was so grateful that in 1865 she commissioned the stained glass window in the stairhall of the east wing, which – perhaps uniquely – portrays patron and architect in adjacent lights.

Elizabethan

The last significant work to be carried out at a gentry house in Lancashire was neither Classical nor Gothic, but was once again given motifs from the reign of Queen Elizabeth. This is the West Wing of 1875 at **Holker**, which was designed by Paley and Austin for William Cavendish, the seventh Duke of Devonshire, to replace a building which had been gutted by a fire [6.20]. It is probably their finest house and forms an interesting contrast to the adjacent wing; this had been designed by George Webster for Cavendish in 1840 (before he inherited his title) in the Tudorbethan manner and rendered with 'Roman' cement. The new work is faced with pink sandstone ashlar and, though of much the same height, has only two – not three – storeys plus attics, and is much more boldly modelled, with bigger windows, a bulbous bay and a prominent tower. Inside, the suite of grand reception rooms – library, drawing room, billiards room and dining room – is richly decorated with imposing fireplaces, panelled walls and plaster ceilings, recalling somewhat those at Levens and Gawthorpe. Holker is also very much a house of its time in the high proportion of the floor plan which is dedicated to communal circulation space: the ground-floor main hall and first-floor gallery, which are linked by a superb timber open-well staircase, are not much narrower than the rooms which lead off them.

6.19. Scarisbrick Hall: the east wing, as strikingly remodelled by Edward Pugin, using medieval motifs but with no attempt to create an apparently genuine medieval building.

'Gentry Houses' for newly-rich families

The succession of decorative styles displayed in gentry houses proper can also be seen in the many smaller houses, built by men who had made their money recently in trade or industry. None of these houses is worth more than a short detour, but one of the most attractive of such houses, and also one of the earliest, is **Stubbylee Hall** (now offices of Rossendale Borough Council) which stands within its large garden, now Stubbylee

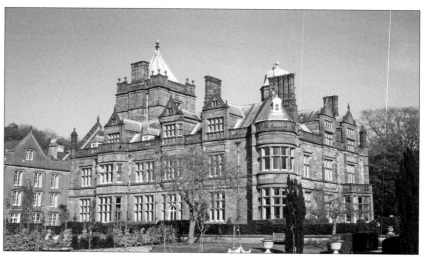

6.20. Holker Hall: Paley and Austin's boldly modelled New Wing and tower of 1873, with a glimpse of George Webster's more restrained 1840s wing on the far left.

Park in **Bacup** [6.2]. It was built in 1809 for James Holt, a baize manufacturer. Its symmetrical façade is seven bays wide and two storeys high, and the two outer bays stand within shallow bows with pilasters at the corners. Its doorway is flanked by Greek Ionic columns.

Oak Hill Park House at **Accrington** (now an Abbeyfield home and private) was built in 1815 for Thomas Hargreaves, the owner of a local calico printing works; it has a plan which is deeper than it is wide and a simple, symmetrical five-bay, two-storey façade graced by a plain pediment. **Ryelands House** in **Skerton** (now offices) was built in 1836 for John Dunn, a coachbuilder who had twice been the Mayor of Lancaster [6.21]. It has a similar plan and, although its main façade has overhanging

6.21. Lancaster, Ryelands House: a suburban villa with a Greek porch for a former coachbuilder and mayor.

eaves rather than a pediment, it has a porch with four approximately Doric columns. The house was much extended by Paley and Austin in 1883, after it had become the suburban home of James Williamson.

All of these Classical houses were built for men who had made their money in trade or industry, for to them a Classical style had overtones of hard work and integrity. They had few delusions about the origins of their families and felt no shame at making a name by their own efforts, rather than by inheriting a title; on the contrary, most were proud of their rise in status. Lady Clifton, a baronet's daughter, complained in 1868 to her husband's agent at Lytham about their lack of deference: 'We have the misfortune', she wrote, 'to belong to a county where merchants and wealth are far above, in their own opinion, the aristocracy and old landed gentry'.[12] To a large extent they were right: industry and trade were rapidly overtaking land as the major source of the nation's wealth. New money was replacing ancient riches.

However, men who had made their money in professions, like the law or medicine, which the gentry might just have recognised as gentlemanly, often chose to have their houses tricked out with Gothic or Tudorbethan details. **Storrs Hall**, near Arkholme (a <u>private</u> house, but visible from a footpath) was designed in 1848, probably by George Webster, for Francis Pearson, a Kirkby Lonsdale solicitor who had just bought the property. It replaced an older house on the site [6.22]. The five-bay, two-storey entrance façade is symmetrical and has mullioned and transomed windows and dormers in the attics; there is also a tower.

As attractive, but more accessible, is what is now the **Greaves Park** restaurant in **Lancaster**, which was finished – possibly to the designs of Edmund Sharpe – in 1843 [6.23]. It was built for Samuel Simpson, a solicitor and the son of a Lancaster merchant.[13] The garden façade is symmetrical with five bays, of which the two outer ones appear as

6.22. Storrs Hall: a Tudorbethan villa in the country, with a tower, built for a well-established solicitor.

6.23. Lancaster, Greaves Park: a suburban Tudorbethan villa for a local solicitor.

cross-wings with a tall bay-window, but the entrance front is merely balanced, with a stair-turret to the left of the doorway and a chimneybreast on the right. All the main windows have mullions and transoms. The interior has been somewhat altered, but the original layout can still be seen: the entrance leads through a vaulted porch and along a passage to the stairhall on the left, with three reception rooms on the right; most of the rooms still have attractive cornices.

These Gothick or Tudorbethan houses were in part public relations exercises, and their particular message was to suggest that either the site or the family was ancient – or, of course, both. In some cases this was justified: Broughton Tower and Capernwray Hall were certainly the seats of old-established families. In other cases the claim was less well-founded: Leighton Hall was an old house Gothicised for a former businessmen, while Storrs Hall was new-built on an old site for a solicitor. The most surprising example of this genealogical make-believe is **Wray Castle** [6.24]. (Its grounds belong to the National Trust and are open to the public.) This extravaganza of battlemented towers and iron-framed arrow-loops, which stands above the western shore of Windermere on a site with a magnificent view, was designed in the 1840s by J.J. Lightfoot for James Dawson, a Liverpool surgeon. He was the son of a former mayor of Liverpool and a brother of the financier, Pudsey Dawson, who inherited **Hornby Castle** (a private house) from a relative at much the same time and had it Gothicised by Sharpe and Paley in 1848. It is tempting to think of sibling rivalry, and this may also have been the case at the pleasantly Classical house, **Clifton Hill** near Forton (private, but just visible from the road), which Robert Gillow, brother of Richard Gillow of Leighton, designed for himself in 1820.

6.24. Wray Castle: a Lake District castle for a former Liverpool surgeon.

Restorations

With the exception of Stubbylee and Clifton Hill, many of these houses pretended to some extent to be what they were not, but a few houses in the nineteenth century became again what they had once been, as their owners restored them to their former glory – or beyond. The first such work had taken place at **Rufford Old Hall** as early as 1724, when the timber-framed cross-wing from Holmeswood Hall was brought to replace the service wing of the medieval house. Restoration – always of pre-Georgian houses – was, however, a largely nineteenth-century activity, and Rufford again provides an early example. Between 1820 and 1825 the cross-wing was renovated, and the 1662 wing was extended, to provide fitting accommodation for the eldest son of the squire, who himself lived at Rufford New Hall, which had been built in the 1760s. The medieval hall was fitted out as a billiards room, with a skylight made to look like a louvre. The 1820s also saw work at **Levens Hall,** when it became a family seat again after nearly a century as a dower house. A tower had been built in 1807, many windows were tidied up and repaired, and attractive 'Elizabethan' plaster ceilings and panelling with Corinthian pilasters were introduced in the library and some bedrooms. Speke Hall too was quite heavily restored in the 1850s.

An interesting example of restoration is **Turton Tower**, which was refurbished and extended in the 1840s by a local textile manufacturer, John Kay, who had long cherished the ambition of being the lord of the manor [6.25]. Much of what visitors now see at the house was done for him: the window sills in the tower were lowered, the service wing to the north was part-clad in stonework with curving 'Dutch' gables and later

6.25. Turton Tower: a photograph of *c*.1880, showing the Elizabethan house, as highly and picturesquely restored for a local textile manufacturer.

part-raised by another storey of 'timber framing'; and the staircase tower was widened. The interior of the house is also largely an attractive Early Victorian confection, but much of the work used old materials, like the original staircase balustrade, the Jacobean panelling in the drawing room, and the late-seventeenth-century panelling in the dining room which was salvaged from the nearby Middleton Hall, when it was demolished in 1844.

The most revealing example of the attitude of mind behind much Victorian restoration is at **Gawthorpe**, where work was done for Sir James Kay-Shuttleworth. He had been a doctor in Manchester and then campaigned successfully to involve the government in primary education; on his retirement he was rewarded for this future-oriented work with a baronetcy. His wife was the Shuttleworth heiress, Janet, and in 1849 they commissioned Charles Barry to refurbish their house, which had been kept in good repair – there are a few rainwater hoppers dated 1732 – but hardly used by the family for two centuries. However, whereas in 1600 the Shuttleworths had wanted a modern house to declare their success and advertise their new-found status, in 1850 the Kay-Shuttleworths wanted to confirm their status by stressing the age of their house.

Barry improved the entrance and then refashioned the hall, which became the dining room. The former dining chamber was henceforth used as the drawing room. The 'parallel-passage' and the gallery above it are partly Jacobean, but the most striking feature of the dining room is the fireplace with its Minton tiles and its tall chimneypiece, carried on

Doric columns; it is decorated with the initials K and S and the coats of arms of the four heiresses who had enriched the Shuttleworths during the centuries. The flues from most of the fireplaces were re-routed from the centre of the house to chimneys in the outside walls.

Barry also designed the fine cantilever staircase which rises to the second floor, from where a narrower stair leads to the tower. Barry raised the tower by another storey, because the Kay-Shuttleworths wanted to believe that their house had been built in Elizabethan times around a medieval peel-tower, rather as at Borwick. There are indeed thick walls near the centre of the house, but nineteenth-century plans show that in fact they contained all of the original chimney flues, which had risen to form a fine display of fashionable chimneys above the stair tower. [3.3] When the Kay-Shuttleworths tried to gild the lily by emphasising the tower, they nearly killed the flower. Before work could continue, the builders had to add two tall buttresses against the back of the house –

6.26. Gawthorpe Hall: the raised tower and the pair of buttresses which prevented its collapse.

where most visitors do not see them [6.26]. In the words of the clerk of works, they had a near escape, but face was saved, and the tower does look fine above the house. Its parapet is inscribed with the Shuttleworths' traditional motto 'Justitia et Prudentia', and one in a pseudo-medieval English, which reads KYND KYNN KNAWNE KEPE. The same motto, which is said to mean 'Kind Friends Know and Keep' and must allude to James Kay's surname, is also to be seen at his shooting lodge, Barbon Manor in Cumbria.

Major restoration work was also carried out at **Hoghton Tower**, which had been neglected after the family took up residence around 1750 at Walton Hall, nearer to the social centre of the county in Preston. For a century the old house was tenanted by cotton weavers and was therefore, like Gawthorpe, spared from any rebuilding in Georgian times. However, by the 1850s, the family must have felt that their seat was too near the increasingly industrial town of Preston and so they moved back to the country in 1862. Work was begun in 1863 under the control of Graham Paley, and completed in 1901 by R.D. Oliver of London. It was slowly, carefully and conservatively done: the ballroom was new, but in keeping; elsewhere, in and out, one must look closely to see the newer panelling and stonework – the illusion of seventeenth-century work is almost complete. Careful work was also done to restore Ordsall Hall in the 1890s, Hall i' th' Wood around 1900 and Borwick Hall after 1910.

Vernacular-style houses for newly-rich families

Almost at the end of the century architects, working now exclusively for newly-rich clients, began to design largish new houses in the country using once again motifs, and plans, from the vernacular tradition, which had been superseded in the later seventeenth century and 'rediscovered' in the 1850s. These houses, often – but rather loosely – called 'Arts and Crafts' houses, must have allowed an agreeably comfortable present while evoking pleasant feelings of a traditional, craft-based past. However, the decorative details were normally designed by the architects, rather than created in the traditional manner by the craftsmen, as they produced their work.

A pleasing house of this period is **Bailrigg House** (now private offices for Lancaster University) [6.27]. It was built in 1902 for Herbert Storey, Lord Ashton's principal commercial rival in Lancaster, to the designs of Woolfall and Eccles of Liverpool. Much as Ashton had done in 1874 by buying Ryelands, so Storey's father had bought the Bailrigg estate in 1887, and his son built a new house some ten years later. The walls and tall chimneys are built of brick, but all its many gables are 'timber-framed', to evoke a pre-industrial past for a rich Victorian industrialist. The pretence is increased by the fact that local bylaws did not allow external timbers to be structural, so they are merely decorative, fixed to the underlying

6.27. Bailrigg House the garden façade of the home of a local factory owner, with tall chimneys and apparent timber-framing.

brickwork. The house is entered on the east side, so that the panelled reception rooms face the afternoon sun and enjoy a fine view over Morecambe Bay to the Lakeland hills. The spacious hall is, as in the Middle Ages, the heart and hub of the house – the first room seen, a space linked to all other rooms on the ground floor, but also where people could gather around a generous fireplace.

More attractive is **Broadleys**, which stands long and low and superbly sited above the east bank of Windermere. It is now the clubhouse of the Windermere Motor Boat Club, but is occasionally open to the public. It was built in 1899 as a week-end and summer retreat for the Yorkshire colliery owner, Arthur Currer-Briggs, to the designs of Charles Voysey. It is entered through a gabled porch in the corner of the front courtyard, where the house stands on the left and the service wing on the right – their pebble-dashed walls dominated by the sweep of their roofs. The front door leads directly to the central hall, which rises through two fairly low storeys and is warmed by a wide inglenook fireplace; here stood a billiard table, which spectators could see from a gallery which also serves as the corridor to the bedrooms. The hall is lit by a large two-storey bow-window [6.28], and there are similar windows for the former drawing room on the left and the dining room on the right – and for the bedrooms above both of them, from which one can enjoy breathtaking views over the lake towards the Langdale Pikes in the North West. (Voysey also designed some miners' cottages and a village institute near Currer-Briggs' colliery at Whitwood, near Castleford; and, thanks to his concerns, the servants' bedrooms at Broadleys were placed above the service wing so that they too could enjoy good views.)

Close to Broadleys is **Blackwell**, which has been beautifully restored by the Lakeland Arts Trust to contain both period rooms and exhibition galleries. It promotes itself as 'The Arts and Crafts House'. Blackwell was designed by Hugh Baillie Scott as a holiday home for Sir Edward Holt, a brewer and later Lord Mayor of

6.28. Broadleys: the garden façade of the Lakeside holiday home for a colliery owner from West Yorkshire.

6.29. Blackwell: the hall with its large inglenook fireplace in the Lakeside holiday home of a Manchester industrialist.

Manchester, and was finished in 1901. As at Broadleys, some of the main rooms enjoy fine views over Windermere, this time westwards to the Coniston Fells. From the outside [6.0] it is a somewhat gaunt, many-gabled house with pebble-dashed walls, but is more welcoming inside. Visitors now go in through what was the servants' entrance; the original porch (to the right) leads across a corridor to the spacious hall [6.29] which is the heart of the house. It is dominated by hand-crafted structural timberwork which provides small 'rooms' within the main space – window seats, a settle from which people could watch the

6.30. Blackwell: the delicately decorated drawing room.

.31. Accrington,
Iaworth Art Gallery:
 nearly symmetrical
 udorbethan home
 or a local cotton
 nanufacturer.

6.31. Accrington, Haworth Art Gallery: a nearly symmetrical Tudorbethan home for a local cotton manufacturer.

billiard table, a cavernous inglenook fireplace and, above it, a 'minstrels' gallery'. Beyond it is the half-panelled dining room with a beamed ceiling and a similar fireplace, while, to the right down the corridor, which runs the length of the house, is the very different and beautiful drawing room, which enjoys the best views over the lake. Its panelling and plasterwork frieze and ceiling are painted white – to hint that this is the ladies' domain – and its fireplace incorporates a glazed display cabinet framed by slender columns with carved capitals, which support the broad mantel-shelf running around the room. [6.30]

At the opposite end of our area is another art gallery, the **Haworth Art Gallery** in **Accrington**, which has a large and fine collection of Tiffany glass. It was built in 1909 as a suburban home in a large garden with sweeping views over the moors for William Haworth, a local cotton manufacturer, and his sister, Anne. Their architect was Walter Brierley of York, and he reverted to the more nostalgic Tudorbethan manner [6.31]. The exterior has a nearly symmetrical entrance façade with gables, bays, mullioned and transomed windows, and a porch with superimposed classical pilasters. Inside, the hall is the hub of the house, from which the fine open-well staircase, the drawing room and dining room (with a deep inglenook fireplace) lead off; and also the billiards room, in which people could watch the game from a generously-sized dais, divided from the room by a screen carried on Ionic columns. Everywhere there are attractive plaster ceilings and panelling, and, inside and out, it is reminiscent of Gawthorpe, which too had been built for a newly-rich family three centuries before – but in a then 'modern' style.

References

1   N. and P. Dalziel, *Kirkby Lonsdale and District in Old Photographs* (1996) pp. 152–3.

2   Robert Kerr, *The Gentleman's House* (1864), p. 173.

3   Pamela A. Sambrook, in *The Country House Servant* (1999), especially in chapter 9, gives some interesting examples.

4   Quoted in Neil Burton, 'Thomas Hopper – the Drama of Eclecticism' in *The Architectural Outsiders* (ed. R. Brown) (1985), p. 114.

5   John Champness, *Thomas Harrison, Georgian Architect of Chester and Lancaster* (2005), pp. 40–44 and 49–54.

6   J. Marsden, 'New Light on Old Masters' in *The Georgian,* Autumn-Winter 2002.

7   B.M. Copeland, *Whittington – the Story of a Country Estate* (1981)

8   Mark Girouard, 'Scarisbrick Hall, Lancashire' in *Country Life* (13.3.1958), p. 507.

9   Peter de Figueiredo and Julian Treuherz, *Cheshire Country Houses* (1988), pp. 131–4.

10 Clare Hartwell (*pers. comm.*).

11 G. Rogers, *Social and Economic Change on Lancashire Landed Estates during the Nineteenth Century, with special reference to the Clifton Estate 1832–1916*, unpublished PhD thesis (Lancaster University, 1981), p. 33 – quoted in J. K. Walton, *Lancashire: A Social History 1558–1939* (1987), p. 135.

12 His obituary, in the *Lancaster Gazette* of 9 July 1881, p. 5, relates these facts.

1. Bispham Hall: near to death in 1986, because of neglect, decay, fire-damage and further neglect; the
ouse was, however, repaired and restored in the 1990s.

7.2. Claughton Hall: a much-changed house which dominates its environment.

CHAPTER SEVEN

Gentry Houses in the Twentieth Century

Introduction

In 1974–75 the Victoria and Albert Museum organised an exhibition, entitled *The Destruction of the Country House 1875–1975*, to mark European Architectural Heritage Year. It seemed like a retrospective, dedicated to the memory of houses which had been demolished in the previous hundred years. As I remember it, their names – some 1100 of them – were read out in a solemn voice, like a roll-call of the dead, to form a sort of audible wallpaper to the exhibition. There were 55 names from Lancashire, a tally only surpassed by the 68 from Yorkshire, which was then three times larger than the County Palatine. The twentieth century appeared to have been an age of unremitting gloom, of death and destruction. This had also been the view back in 1935 when Osbert Sitwell wrote in his Foreword to Ralph Dutton's classic book, *The English Country House*: 'What country houses of any size, one wonders, can hope to survive the next fifty years?'

We now know, with hindsight, that his view was too pessimistic, and that Heritage Year, doubtless thanks to the exhibition, was the turning point to an upswing of the fortunes of country houses in England. More than half of the pages of the book with the same title,[1] which accompanied the exhibition, show photographs of houses which had disappeared, but the book also contains essays – seven on specific houses and twice as many on general topics – which strike a soberly optimistic note. Those seven houses – none is in Lancashire – have survived for a further thirty-six years, and so have almost all of the gentry houses in Lancashire which existed in 1975.

Many of these surviving gentry houses, though, have lost their link with the landowning family which built or rebuilt them, and with the estates which supported them, and this is a source of sorrow to many people. However, the houses themselves survive physically – as often as not in better condition than at any time since before 1914, thanks largely to their adaptation to new uses. Some have not just survived, but have been brought back from a near-death experience [7.1].

This chapter is short, because the story of gentry house building in Lancashire simply stops just after the middle of the twentieth century. There are now no landowners who wield significant political power, even at the local level, and no land-owning family has built a significant house here, or even remodelled an old one, for nearly fifty years. The most recent one was the New House, designed by Claude Phillimore for the Earl of Derby and built in 1963–4 in the grounds of Knowsley Hall. However, while this chapter starts with decline and demolitions, it continues with survivals, and has a postscript which talks of revivals.

Builders – the gentry in decline

The twentieth century was not a period in which gentry families found it easy to have the confidence in the future which inspires people to invest in fine new buildings.

The decline in the gentry's power and influence had begun, however, in the middle of the nineteenth century and was merely accelerated by the declining prosperity of British agriculture towards the end. By definition, gentry houses were built and maintained from the profits of agriculture; consequently, when these declined, as steamships and refrigerators made it possible from the late 1880s to bring to this country American wheat, New Zealand lamb and Argentinian beef at prices lower than those of local producers, the maintenance of existing houses was reduced, and few new ones were built. Landowners nationally were hit by a depression in the agricultural economy, which was widely regarded as a disaster. The *Estates Gazette* claimed in 1892 that 'Men who have made money and by judicious investment are getting from 3½ to 4½ per cent on their spare capital now seem but little disposed to take on themselves the ownership of land, to get at best a return of 2½ per cent'. In 1895 Oscar Wilde put it more wittily, when Lady Bracknell said in *The Importance of being Earnest* that land 'gives one position, but prevents one keeping it up'. In fact, that position was already under threat, in Lancashire especially – as Lady Clifton (see p. 149) had seen in 1868 – from men making their money from trade and industry.

The agricultural depression hit the mainly arable areas of the country harder than the largely pastoral ones, and many landowners in Lancashire, where much of the usable land is suitable for dairying or for market gardening, were able to diversify into producing food for the growing populations of Liverpool, Manchester, Preston and Burnley. Such diversification, however, demanded considerable investment from a reduced income before any profits could be made.[2]

There was as well another price to pay. While some gentlemen who owned land in these growing urban areas found their ground rents increasing year by year – between 1876 and 1900, for example, the annual rental income of the Earls of Derby (much of it from Liverpool) rose from £160,000 to £300,000 – the very proximity of growing industrial towns made farming less viable, because of trespassing and damage in many places, and made life less pleasant for the gentry families who had to live there. Some gentlemen in such areas let their houses to middle-class tenants. This happened near Rochdale: Castleton Hall, which had previously been rented by a local MP, came onto the market in 1889 – just when my great-grandfather, Rev. Thomas Champness, was looking for a house to accommodate a training college for Methodist lay preachers [7.3]. He leased it for fourteen years, but this respite was only temporary, and the Hall – a many-gabled house of about 1600 with a large wing of 1719 – was pulled down in 1905.[3] Other Lancashire families moved away entirely, selling their houses and the parks in which they stood for use by the local authority This happened at Heaton in 1901, at Towneley in 1902, and at Platt in 1906. Trafford Park, next to the new Manchester Ship Canal, had been sold in 1896 and became the site of the world's first industrial estate well before the First World War.

The worst of the agricultural depression had been weathered by 1900, but there was no Edwardian heyday, thanks in part to the impact of 'death-duties' on wealthy land-owning families. This tax on the value of an inherited estate had been introduced by a Conservative government as far back as 1894, but was increased by the Liberals after much bitter debate in 1909 as part of Lloyd George's 'People's Budget'. In 1913 therefore the new Earl of Crawford had to pay taxes of £103,000, on an estate whose annual income was valued at £321,000, whereas in 1880 his father had paid no more than £10,000.[4] The 'People's Budget' led as well to the Parliament Act of 1911, which reduced the powers of the House of Lords and therefore the political influence of the 'landed interest'.

7.3. Castleton Hall in its last heyday – home for the 'Joyful News' evangelists between 1889 and 1903.

Then came the First World War. Every community was hard hit by the deaths on the fields of Flanders, to an extent which is almost unimaginable today. The roll call on the 1914–18 war memorial behind Lancaster Town Hall, for example, shows 1010 names, including 63 sets of brothers, out of what had been a total population of 41,410 according to the 1911 census. The gentry were in no way exempt. War memorials in many village churches show the names of sons of the 'big house', and A.J.P. Taylor, who was no sycophant, stated in his *English History 1914–45* that 'casualties were about three times heavier in proportion among junior officers than with common soldiers'.[5] Many landed estates were left without an heir.

The emotional problems of untimely deaths were compounded by the fact that, in many cases, when the duties had to be paid, agricultural prices, which had been guaranteed by Act of Parliament during the war to encourage production, fell after the Act was repealed in 1921. Rents were low, and labour costs were higher, so there was little incentive to invest in land, and, despite a slumping market, many families saw no alternative to selling up and moving away. It has been calculated that between 1918 and 1921 a quarter of England changed hands.[6] The Ainsworth family, which had bought the Smithills estate in 1801, sold it to Bolton County Borough Council in 1938. A precedent had been set in 1922 when Reginald Tatton, whose seat was Cuerden Hall, gave the Hall at Astley, and sold the surrounding park, to Chorley Borough Council as a war memorial and museum.

The last gentry houses

A number of houses disappeared after the First World War. The most striking case was that of the timber-framed Agecroft Hall, near Pendlebury, which was not wholly lost but was taken down beam by beam and moved in 1926 to Richmond in the USA. At Halsnead Park, near Prescot, the Willis family moved away to the Midlands, demolished the house in 1932 and opened a colliery in its park. The most grievous loss was at Lathom House, where the main block of the house was demolished in 1922, and the estate was sold to pay off the debts of the last Earl of Lathom. To crown it all, the family's superb archives were simply burnt at a colliery in Skelmersdale. Lathom was, though, far from being the only Georgian house to be demolished between the wars; the disquiet at this 'onslaught' among members of what is now the Society for the Protection of Ancient Buildings led to the formation in 1937 of the Georgian Group – to encourage appreciation of Georgian buildings and to campaign for their protection. Another dozen gentry houses in Lancashire also disappeared before 1939. In so far as they were replaced, it was with 'suburban' houses in large gardens for recently wealthy families – continuing a pattern that had developed in the late nineteenth century.

Such a house was **Eaves Hall** at West Bradford (now a country hotel) which was rebuilt in 1922 [7.4]. There had been a house on the site since 1871, built by John Burton, who came from a family of prosperous cotton spinners near Manchester. This house was remodelled in an extensive garden, with little concern about costs, by his nephew, Arthur Burton. His architects, Hitchon and Pickup of Burnley, enlarged the old house and re-fronted it in brick with Portland stone dressings, in a grand but slightly pompous manner, which was reminiscent of the works of Wren and was fashionable for public buildings. The two-storey entrance façade has slightly projecting wings linked by a portico of coupled Tuscan columns, supporting a balcony in front of an elaborate stone-faced centrepiece with an open pediment carried on coupled Ionic columns. The entrance door leads to a spacious but fairly low panelled hall, which gives access to the stairhall and all the main rooms. The house had garages for six cars; it was given a telephone connection in 1923, but had to generate its own electricity until 1932.

A stranger example of the re-modelling of an older house with new money – in a vernacular rather than a Classical manner – can be seen in the Lune valley. **Claughton Hall** used to stand opposite the parish church on the A683. A wing still stands there, but between 1931 and 1935, the Manchester architect, Harry S. Fairhurst, had the twin-towered, many-windowed bulk of the house moved up the hill and re-built, with the addition of a hall based on crucks from a farm in Herefordshire [7.2 and 7.5]. It is private, but can be seen in the distance from the main road and

7.4. Eaves Hall – rebuilding in the Wrenaissance manner.

7.5. Claughton Hall – rebuilt and enlarged in a vernacular manner on its new site.

also from Hornby Castle. This was doubtless deliberate – shades of Gawthorpe! – for it allowed the owner, Esmond Morse, the managing director of Lord Ashton's company, to look down towards, and outstare, the owner – by then another industrialist – of the older, single-towered house, which had hitherto dominated the landscape.

More so than the First World War, the Second sounded the knell of the gentry house.[7] Eaves Hall, which Arthur Burton had sold at a great loss in 1930, was bought for use as out-of-London offices by the tea company, Brooke Bond. Rigmaden Park, near Kirkby Lonsdale, which had been built in the 1820s for a Kendal banker, housed an evacuated school. Many country houses were requisitioned for the armed forces. Some, like Lytham Hall, accommodated hospitals and convalescent homes; others were used for billeting servicemen – 133,516 young men were housed at Heaton before they went for flying training overseas. Ordsall was used as a wireless station. Some houses were well looked-after and survived the war; others were less fortunate. Staff at Bank Hall near Bretherton protected the western approaches to Liverpool, but took little care of the house, which gradually fell into decay. Much the same was true of Woodfold Hall, near Blackburn, and of Clayton Hall, near Accrington, which were not re-occupied after the war. Buckshaw Hall and Worden Old Hall were enclosed within the precinct of the Royal Ordnance Factory near Euxton in 1937, after which they were used as offices for thirty years and then neglected for as long again – but they have now been refurbished as part of the redevelopment of the ROF site.

Many houses were simply left to decay quietly, hidden behind walls or up long tracks, out of the sight and mind of the local authorities who, the owners rightly believed, lacked the will to do, or pay, anything to stop the process. Local authorities after World War II had a mixed record. The Borough of Colne demolished Alkincoats, rather than repair the roof, and the City of Manchester allowed Baguley Hall to rot for decades. It is fair, though, to add that most voters wanted taxes to be reduced and were happy to take part in a Dutch auction on local-authority rates. On the other hand, while new building was still tightly constrained in the late 1940s and early '50s, some local authorities did buy country houses in good condition for use as colleges or special schools. Alston Hall, Broughton Tower, Hopwood Hall near Rochdale (whose owners had left in the 1920s), Singleton Hall and Wennington Hall were all saved in this way.

So too was Scarisbrick Hall, which later provided an interesting case. In 1946 it had been bought from the family for use as a teachers' training college, but the college closed in 1963. The Hall and its grounds were bought by a local company, which intended to demolish the house carefully, for the sake of its fine materials, and build an estate of new houses on the site. If the company had succeeded, there would now be a significant hole in the history of English architecture, but – fortunately – the then Conservation Officer of Lancashire County Council, Tom Pennington, was able to persuade the Ministry of Housing and Local Government that the house was of such importance that it should be listed. (The listing of buildings of special architectural or historic interest had begun towards the end of the war – as part of the reconstruction effort – in order to identify those buildings which deserved to be protected from harmful changes.) Tom Pennington's case was supported by the Victorian Society, which had been founded in 1958 to encourage the appreciation and protection of buildings, which it had hitherto been fashionable to despise. (There is now also the Twentieth Century Society, founded with similar aims.)

Once Scarisbrick Hall was listed, demolition was impossible, and so the company put the house back on the market. It was later bought for use as a school, but the new owners did not want to buy a number of paintings and carved panels, which were fixtures (and therefore part of the house's fabric) but had been sold before the house was listed. The company insisted that the County Council should buy them, and the law was on the company's side. The Council did not dispute the case, paid what was then a sizeable bill, and now possesses some fine works of art in a building which it does not own. It is an anomalous situation, but has worked amicably.

Another success story in the same corner of Lancashire, and at the same time, was the remodelling and extension of Meols Hall. It was not an entirely isolated example, for a handful of other landowning families were rebuilding their houses – but on a reduced scale. However, with the exception of Dalton Hall near Burton-in-Kendal, which has been described and illustrated,[8] they are inaccessible to the public. At Dalton,

Clough Williams-Ellis replaced a rambling Victorian house, riddled with dry rot, with a smaller house – rather like a Georgian doll's house; it was his last work, in 1968.

Meols Hall, near Southport, is, however, more interesting than any of them [7.6]. Its owner/designer, Roger Hesketh, who had studied architecture and appreciated Palladio, had long cherished the hope of making something of this old family property, whose estate he finally inherited in 1938. The war and the consequent restrictions on new building put paid to these plans, and Hesketh's service as an MP delayed them further until 1959.

The design of the new house at Meols was constrained by the wish to retain two seventeenth-century features – the centre of the entrance façade and the gabled wing on its right – and also the wish to display a large collection of family portraits and other paintings, which Hesketh had inherited from a cousin. The dimensions and decorative details of the single-storey library, whose bow-window is visible on the front of the house, were determined by the width of the fine Regency bookcase, which came from Bold Hall (a house by Leoni, which had been demolished around 1900) and by the height of a life-size portrait of an Arab stallion.

The drawing room, garden room and dining room form an attractive sequence of interconnected spaces on the back of the house; they face the garden, which is flanked by two gazebos, modelled on the one remaining at Rossall, which belonged to the Hesketh family in the nineteenth century. The garden façade, with its slightly recessed centre, dates from the 1960s but looks much older [7.7]; it has the vertical emphasis and taller proportions associated with early Georgian houses, and its bricks came from the eighteenth-century Tulketh Hall in Preston, and its

7.6. Meols Hall: the largely seventeenth-century entrance front, with the library of 1960 to the left.

.7. Meols Hall: the
arden front, largely
f the 1960s but built
1 an Early Georgian
1anner.

classical doorcase from Lathom House. The building work was done, not
by a contractor but by local craftsmen under the supervision of the owner
– a deliberate return to the old ways, which turned out well.

In his work at Meols, Hesketh was helped by his brother, Peter
Fleetwood-Hesketh, who had also studied architecture, but is better
known as the author of *Murray's Lancashire Architectural Guide*. This was
published in 1955, but is still the best single-volume book on the County's
historic buildings.

Both inside and out, Meols Hall, with its combination of old and new,
good furniture and family portraits, is an appropriate place to finish the
story of gentry housing in Lancashire.[9] There is nothing here to compare
with two more recent houses in Cheshire – Eaton Hall, which was built
in 1972 in a starkly Modern style, and then remodelled with a mansard
roof in 1990; or Henbury Hall, which was built in 1986 to a design
which, with its dome and four porticos, looks fairly like the famous Villa
Capra near Vicenza, designed in 1552 by Andrea Palladio.[10]

New uses for old houses

Meols Hall was the last significant gentry house to be built in Lancashire,
but only marks the end of part of the story. Since World War II many
houses, built for gentry families, have found new owners and new uses
and have secured thereby a new lease of life.

Many survive without their estates, which were sold off separately.
Some of them are still private houses, like Burrow Hall. Others have been
converted to flats, as at Alkrington Hall and Broughton Tower; and
several gentry houses also contain flats for people who are not members

of the family. Birchley Hall and Cuerden Hall accommodate Sue Ryder homes; Gisburne Park Hall has become a hospital, and Ince Blundell Hall a convalescent home. Rufford New Hall was used as a hospital for about thirty years, but was then remodelled in the early 1990s as part of a big housing estate.

Some successes were the result of the initiative of private individuals, like the rehabilitation after decades of neglect of Bispham Hall [7.1] near Billinge, New Hall at Clayton-le-Dale, Parbold Hall and Thurnham Hall. Somewhat similarly, Rigmaden Hall and Woodfold Hall have been remodelled within their original walls. Clayton Hall near Accrington was even demolished in 1986, and then the centre was rebuilt soon after, as closely as possible to the original external design. An important factor at Bispham was the involvement of the Vivat Trust; similarly, the Landmark Trust was involved with Lancaster City Council in the restoration of the Music Room in Lancaster.

Other successes came about after the activity of private companies, as when the Guardian Assurance Company foreclosed the mortgage on Lytham Hall and acquired it and 800 hectares in 1965. It then used the house for hospitality and office purposes for thirty years and paid for the necessary restoration work by selling off some land for housing on the southern and western boundary of the estate. Other successes involved a local authority, as when Lancashire County Council challenged the readiness of Hyndburn Borough Council to demolish Oak Hill Park House at Accrington in 1989; we won.

One of the biggest groups of houses with new uses is formed by those which have become local authority museums – at Accrington, Hall i' th' Wood, Heaton, Ordsall, Platt, Rawtenstall (a house built in 1840 by the owner of New Hall Hey Mill), Smithills, Towneley and Turton. And that is not to mention Gawthorpe Hall, Rufford Old Hall, Sizergh Castle and Speke Hall, which belong to the National Trust. Lytham Hall, meanwhile, was bought in 1997 from Guardian Royal Exchange by a local trust with generous help from another local firm, British Aerospace; it is now being managed very positively by the Heritage Trust for the North West, as both an historic house and also a venue for conferences, weddings and other ceremonies.

Ashton Hall, Hall o' th' Hill and Shaw Hill have long been the clubhouses of golf clubs; the last is also an hotel, like Dunkenhalgh and Farington Lodge. Esthwaite Lodge near Hawkshead is a youth hostel, and Samlesbury Hall and Heskin Hall now house antiques showrooms.

Schools have been opened at Scarisbrick and Wennington, and there are religious colleges at Capernwray and Ellel. Bailrigg House contains offices for Lancaster University. Conishead Priory has reverted to its original, pre-Reformation, use as the home of a religious community – albeit for Buddhists, not Christians. But there is, in fact, nothing new in the re-use of redundant gentry houses. Bushell's house in Goosnargh was converted to almshouses in 1745, and fifty years later Stonyhurst became a school.

The future?

The golden age of the gentry is long past and beyond recall. The building of new gentry houses stopped some forty years ago. The era of the political dominance of the landed gentry came to an end more than twice as far back. A dozen or so families, however, still survive in Lancashire in largish houses on largish estates and, locally, enjoy a measure of social prestige and therefore influence – sponsoring charities and accommodating charity events, heading subscription lists and serving on committees. (A few open their houses to the public, notably at Browsholme, Hoghton, Holker, Leighton, Levens and Meols.) These families have, however, no overt political power, except perhaps at the very local level, but they set a good example outside their immediate area.

I have no nostalgia for any period in the past, nor any wish to have lived – let alone to live now – the life of a country landowner in a large inherited house. It is, however, fair to acknowledge that many – perhaps most – of the gentry, despite what we now regard as their faults – their reported arrogance and their disdain for those below them in the social hierarchy – did lead lives which were influenced by the ideals of *noblesse oblige* and by the idea of stewardship of their estates, rather than simple exploitation. It is difficult to believe that many of today's politicians, celebrities and other 'leaders of society' share similar ideals.

But what of the future of the houses themselves? Interest in them has been growing for half a century, thanks largely to the scholarly, though sometimes sycophantic, articles in *Country Life*. Very few gentry houses in England are now owned by the families which first built them, but this process has been going on for centuries. Most of them are no more than the often beautiful shells of a now almost extinct society. Their fabric must, surely, be more important to us now than the link between a family and a house.

As a society, we have changed our collective mind somewhat since that exhibition in 1975. Most of us are not prepared to accept that something of beauty or of special interest should be damaged, let alone destroyed – even to achieve a politically desirable end, if that end can be achieved without such damage and at relatively little extra cost. Most of us believe that buildings which are widely considered to be beautiful – regardless of the continued existence, or not, of the families (or organisations) who created and sustained them – can often, like good music or fine paintings, enhance the lives of people who experience them. Furthermore, in an age which is slowly becoming more 'environmentally conscious', gentry houses are thought by some people – though others dismiss this view as hopelessly Romantic – to have a symbolic value as former centres of the traditional, farming-based economy, in which resources were regarded as assets to be managed sustainably, rather than be mined for short-term profit.

However this may be, somewhere in Lancashire some gentry houses will disappear before the middle of this century – probably because the cost of rehabilitation is prohibitive. The steeply rising price of houses between about 1970 and 2007 encouraged repair and conversion and often made this profitable, but now, at a time of economic uncertainty, this question of the balance between financial cost and heritage benefit must be addressed squarely. I believe and have always believed, that, unless a building is of *truly outstanding* quality, it is not a wise use of ultimately scarce resources to spend, say, a couple of million pounds on its repair and conversion, if it is only worth a million at the end.

Nevertheless, history – which is an inadequate guide to the future but the only one which we have – suggests that, barring national calamities, the most important houses of real architectural quality and historic interest in England will continue to survive physically, though a few more will lose the link to their families and their estates. In these cases the National Trust may perhaps acquire the very best among any which do come onto the market – those which are time-capsules or have the finest architecture and the richest collections and, probably, the best 'downstairs' rooms and service wings. English Heritage may also show an interest. Some houses will be bought by newly wealthy families – as has been the case for the past four hundred years – or they will be used as hotels and conference centres, a modern form of 'old English hospitality'. We can, I believe, be reasonably confident about the medium-term future of gentry houses in Lancashire, the finest part of the County's architectural heritage.

References

1   Roy Strong, Marcus Binney and John Harris, *The Destruction of the Country House* (1974).

2   See chapter 5 of G. Rogers' unpublished PhD thesis (Lancaster University, 1981), *Social and Economic Change on Lancashire Landed Estates during the Nineteenth Century, with special reference to the Clifton Estate 1832–1916*.

3   Its demolition is pictured in a photograph on p. 70 of J. Cole and R. Catlow, *Memory Lane, Rochdale* (2001), and there is also an attractive picture of the Hall in the 1860s on p. 171 of John Martin Robinson's *Guide to the Country Houses of the North West* (1991).

4   C. B. Phillips and J. H. Smith, *Lancashire and Cheshire from AD 1540* (1994), p. 231.

5   A. J. P. Taylor, *English History, 1914–1945* (1965), p. 120.

6   'Estates Gazette', 31. 12. 1921, quoted in Heather A. Clemenson, *English Country Houses and Landed Estates* (1982), p. 111.

7   John Martin Robinson, *The Country House at War* (1989) tells some interesting stories, some about Lancashire houses.

8   John Martin Robinson, *The Latest Country Houses* (1984) pp. 98–100, with a plate opposite p. 128.

9   John Martin Robinson describes it more fully in his *The Latest Country Houses* (1984), pp. 179–185.

10 There is a photograph of Eaton in its original form on the front cover of John Martin Robinson's *The Latest Country Houses* (1984) and of Henbury on the front cover of *Cheshire Country Houses* (1988) by Peter de Figueiredo and Julian Treuherz.

8.1. Samlesbury Hall: two probably fifteenth-century crucks in the hall,
sweeping up from the ground towards the ridge of the roof.

Appendix – Firmness, or Building a Gentry House

Introduction

Building a house was probably the most expensive activity which most gentlemen ever undertook. Few did it more than once in a lifetime and, if they were sensible, they did so only after much thought. Building or modernising a house in the middle of one's estate was always a political statement, a public relations exercise, undertaken in the hope of impressing visitors and inspiring awe among one's social inferiors, envy among one's equals, and grudging respect among one's superiors. Most people in a parish welcomed significant building work at the hall, because it put a lot of money into the local economy. However, a gentleman needed to decide whether the return on the investment – the better accommodation and finer status symbols acquired – would outweigh the costs in terms of money and of the trouble of living on a building site. He needed to think also about the scale of the work: was a new building really necessary, or would an extension suffice? Or would the money be better spent on fashionable clothes and furniture, a fine carriage and horses, a monument in the parish church? Many people during the six centuries covered by this book would have thought that Thomas Fuller's advice, given in 1642, was wise: 'A house had better be too little for a day than too great for a year. And it's easier borrowing of thy neighbour a brace of chambers for a night than a bag of money for a twelvemonth'.[1]

Not everyone took that advice, of course. If an existing house provided sufficient accommodation for the current owner, he was unlikely to change it, but a new owner or life tenant might feel that the house was too small or too old-fashioned. As the nation grew wealthier, and the gentry became more wealthy in relation to most other members of society, so their aspirations were inflated. A father's wants became his son's needs; and houses, which would have passed muster earlier, were felt to be inadequate. Buildings are part of the autobiography of an age.

The new owner might find that he had enough money – from his father's savings, perhaps, or from the dowry provided by his wife. He would, however, still need an appropriate model, a competent designer and skilful craftsmen.

Most of the early-seventeenth-century estate accounts for Gawthorpe survive and include many entries relating to the building of the Hall between 1600 and 1607. They not only allow us to see how that house was built then, but also give a good idea of traditional practice – which was current until around 1900. The house was built by a series of specialist craftsmen under the general control of the owner's steward. (This was the case until architects became common during the eighteenth century, after which a clerk of works, appointed by the architect, took over the responsibility of supervising the construction work.)

Stonemasons began at Gawthorpe by building the foundations and walls, the chimney stacks, doorways and window surrounds. As the outside walls rose, carpenters – who had already provided scaffolding and built shelters for some of the craftsmen – inserted the floor joists and finally raised the roof timbers, which were then covered by slaters and plumbers. After that, inside the house, the floorboards were laid, and joiners framed the doors, the main staircase and panelling, while glaziers made and inserted the windows, sometimes with the aid of smiths who wrought the iron frames for side-hung casements. Finally plasterers finished and decorated the walls and ceilings, working downwards from the top of the house, to reduce the risk of damaging their work; they left by the back door at the end of their contract.[2]

Building involved risks, which we seldom have to face. We can usually buy a house 'off the shelf' and can therefore see what we are getting. Most owners in the past had to build a house on the basis of an idea in a designer's brain and, later, in a few drawings; occasionally, though, gentlemen asked for their house to be modelled on another house elsewhere. They might, however, build what appeared to be an up-to-date house, only to find that fashion was changing – as must have been the case at Platt Hall in the 1760s – or that the perceived drawbacks of the new house outweighed the hoped-for benefits – as, probably, at Gawthorpe 150 years before that. Few men, though, were so soon disillusioned as the first Duke of Westminster: in 1870 he had spent some £600,000 on a new Eaton Hall near Chester and then in 1881 wrote, 'Now that I have built a palace, I wish I lived in a cottage.'[3] His house was demolished in 1963. If builders spent their money too quickly, they would find that they had ample time to repent. But few could sell up the family seat and move away.

Sometimes a house was never finished. A sensible owner built the carcase of his house – the walls and roof – as quickly as possible, with money already saved and available, and then completed it, as necessary, from annual income over the next few years; but some people's ambitions outran their purse. Sometimes too the owner died, while the house was being built, and the work was given up. This happened twice at Allerton Hall in the 1750s, when both the Hardman brothers died, and the house was incomplete for sixty years. It happened once at Parbold Hall after Thomas Crisp died in 1758, and the planned rebuilding is still unfinished.

Building materials

Timber framing

Most medieval gentry houses in the lowland counties of England, which include the western half of Lancashire, were built of prefabricated timber-frames. The timbers for each building were cut to size and loosely fixed together in the carpenter's yard, where the mortice-and-tenon joints were marked for the purposes of identification. The whole frame was then dismantled and transported, beam by beam, to its site and then re-erected, being held together tightly by stout wooden pegs. (There is an interesting exhibition, including scale models, of the techniques of timber framing at Little Moreton Hall.)

Wood is fairly weak in compression – as one can see by pressing a knife blade into a lath. However, provided it is kept dry, wood is strong in tension: it is not difficult to bend a lath, but some force is necessary actually to *break* it. There are obvious limits, and they have practical consequences which one can see in buildings. It is, for instance, rare to find a two-storeyed medieval house – whether of timber or stone – which is wider than about 7 metres (or 24 feet). The main reason for this is simple: in order to span such a distance without sagging under the load of an upper floor, a timber beam must be about 35 cm deep and should be about 15 cm thick to reduce the risk of twisting. (When houses were designed using imperial measurements, a simple formula was used to calculate timber sizes; for example, a beam 24 feet long had to be 24÷2 (=12) + 1 (=13) inches deep.) Timbers of a larger size are not easy to find and are also heavy to handle. A block of oak measuring 30cm each way weighs almost 25 kg. (In imperial terms, a cubic foot weighs about half a hundredweight.)

Timber-framing developed significantly in the Middle Ages, and the earlier technique, using A-shaped pairs of what are called 'cruck-blades', jointed together at the top, was generally superseded – in gentry houses, at least – before 1500 by 'box-frames'. In the system of cruck trusses the weight of a building's roof was supported largely by horizontal beams, called purlins, resting on the backs of the cruck-blades; the upright outer walls themselves were self-supporting but not load-bearing. Cruck frames can give a fine open space – as can be seen in the hall of **Samlesbury Hall**, which was built around 1400 [8.1]. Only two crucks now exist there

8.2. Buckshaw Hall (a photograph of *c.*1980): box frames in a large farmhouse of about 1600. After years of neglect within the former Royal Ordnance Factory near Euxton, the house is now (2011) being refurbished.

in their original form – standing on the ground and meeting at the top – since the others were altered when the wall fireplace was built and the bay-window was added around 1545. A fine cruck-framed barn can also be seen behind **Park Hill,** the Pendle Heritage Centre in Barrowford. However, crucks posed a number of problems. Carpenters needed very large trees, since each pair of crucks was made by splitting a single curved tree-trunk lengthwise; furthermore, the resulting building could not be given a second storey or be easily extended, since the dimensions of the original cruck-blades determined the height and width of the building.

The timber-framed walls of the recently renovated **Buckshaw Hall,** which dates probably from about 1600, show the later structural system [8.2]. Box-frames were technically more sophisticated than crucks: they were more flexible in use, since they could be extended fairly simply and used smaller pieces of straight timber, which were easier to find. Despite this, it took a lot of trees to build even a small house. Basically, the weight of the roof was borne on the horizontal tie-beams of the triangular roof-trusses, whose ends rested on load-bearing outer walls (Before the introduction of tie-beams in the fifteenth century, the rafters of a roof exerted an outward thrust on the walls, as does an arch – see below). These walls were made up of a lattice of posts and rails, pegged together, and were linked at intervals to similarly framed cross-walls carrying the roof-trusses. The squarish spaces between the posts and the rails were each infilled with a panel of woven wattles rendered with mud and straw ('wattle-and-daub') [8.3]; from the seventeenth century this wattle-and-daub infill was often replaced by bricks. In South Lancashire, as in Cheshire and much of the West Midlands, the fashion was to strengthen these frames – not that this was really necessary – with four corner-braces [8.4]. Sometimes these

3.3. Wattle and daub infill in varying states of disrepair.

are merely straight, but often, as at Ordsall, Samlesbury and Smithills, they are specially shaped to provide a decorative motif of quatrefoils.

Masonry – stonework

3.4. Decorative corner braces forming quatrefoil panels.

Timber-framed houses were built by members of the minor gentry until the middle of the seventeenth century in lowland Lancashire, where stone is not easily available. It is, however, difficult to build tall houses from timber, so most middling or major gentry houses after 1550 were built of stonework (or brickwork).

Stone is heavy; it is three times denser than timber, much stronger in compression, but much weaker in tension. A stone wall would have to be two miles high, before the bottom stones disintegrated under the crushing pressure of the weight of those above them, but a piece of stone as thin as a lath can be snapped more easily than a lath. This limitation has practical consequences: openings for doors cannot be much more than a metre wide, unless the lintel stones are very deep and therefore unmanageably heavy. Windows can only be made wider than that, if they are sub-divided

8.5. The timber centring on which an arch could be built.

8.6. (below) An arch without adequate abutment, but where remedial strengthening must have taken place to prevent collapse.

by vertical mullions which can support the lintel. This became traditional practice.

To span an opening more than a metre or so wide, masons in the past – who did not have reinforced concrete lintels at their disposal –needed an arch, whose wedge-shaped stones, called voussoirs, were laid above a timber arch-shaped frame, called a centring [8.5], until the mortar dried. The problem with an arch, though, is that it 'never sleeps'; that is to say that its voussoirs always exert an outward pressure and need adequate abutment at the sides, if the arch is not to deform and – sometimes – collapse [8.6]. So-called 'relieving arches' can be built over wide openings for windows and doors to carry most of the weight of the wall above them, so that a stone lintel needs to do little more than carry its own weight. Such arches can be seen above the windows of the **Judges' Lodgings** in

Lancaster [3.14], but they must have originally been hidden under an external render. Relieving arches were, however, sometimes used decoratively in nineteenth-century work.

Stone walls are always built in two 'leaves' – an inner leaf and an outer leaf [8.7]. Good practice demands that longer 'through stones' are set at intervals at right angles to the face of the wall, so that they have a place in both leaves and thus bind them together. Until the introduction of Portland cement in the mid-nineteenth century stones were bedded in a slow-setting mortar made of lime and sand in the proportions of about 1:3. The purpose of the mortar was not so much to glue the stones together as to fill completely the gaps between them, so that, when the mortar did dry out and harden – a slow chemical process involving the absorption of carbon dioxide from the air to recreate a sort of limestone –the wall was completely solid and monolithic. Whether or not this ideal state would be achieved depended on the skill and care of the craftsmen.

.7. The two leaves ⸱f a stone wall – ⱱithout enough ⱨrough stones.

The inner leaf of a wall bears the load of the timber floors and timber roof trusses. The outer leaf has a double function: it adds mass to the inner leaf and thus – if well built – makes the wall stronger, and it also provides a protective and decorative skin for the building. Traditionally, the inner leaf was often built of what is called random rubble – which is rather like drystone walling plus mortar – but in better work these stones were roughly squared before being laid. In gentry building the outer leaf was always built of better-quality stonework than the inner leaf – with squared rubble laid in courses and without vertical joints running across two courses. The best work, called ashlar, has carefully finished stones, laid in regular courses with very fine joints, to give a smooth surface. (It was, of course, common for main façades to be built of better quality stonework than less conspicuous walls.)

The use of stone (rather than timber-framing) for walls, and of stone or clay tiles (rather than thatch) for roofs, meant that kitchens no longer presented a significant fire-risk and could be accommodated safely within a house. This became the standard practice in Elizabethan times.

Masonry – brickwork

As far as we know, the first use of bricks in a Lancashire gentry house was in the family wing, built around 1545 at **Samlesbury Hall**. This was late by English standards: Little Wenham Hall in Suffolk dates from about 1280. In the seventeenth century bricks came to replace timber-framing as the normal building material in those lowland parts of the county, where stone is not easily available.

Bricks cannot withstand crushing weights as well as stones can and they are also as weak in tension, but, since they seldom weigh more than two to three kg each and are all of roughly the same size, they are easily handled by one man who has a labourer or apprentice to mix and bring some mortar, as required.

Until late in the nineteenth century all bricks were made, as is still the case nowadays with 'hand-made' bricks, by forcing large lumps of prepared clay into wooden moulds, trimming off the top surface, and then firing the 'green' bricks. Early brickmakers had little control over the temperature in their kilns; in consequence bricks were often over-fired or under-fired and therefore irregular in their dimensions. They had to be sorted for quality, and only the better ones were used on the outer faces of the main walls of a building.

If a bricklayer is to build a strong wall, he needs to lay the bricks so that they interlock – or 'bond' – both along the face of a wall and across its depth, with no vertical joints across two courses. (All the brick walls in the houses in this book were built solid. Cavity-walls – with a gap between the leaves for the purposes of damp-proofing – were not generally introduced until about 1900.) In early brickwork the bonding of bricks was rough and ready, but by about 1600 the bricks in the visible face of a wall were normally laid in what we now call English bond, that is with a course of 'stretchers' (bricks placed lengthways) and then, above them, a course of 'headers' (bricks laid end-on) and so on up the wall, as can be seen at **Hough End Hall**. In early-seventeenth-century work bricks whose ends had been over-fired (which produced a black, glass-like texture) were often used, so that these headers created diamond or chevron patterns within the outer face of the finished brickwork. There is a little such work at **Hough End Hall,** and at **Carr House,** Bretherton [3.2], but this rather busy patterning soon fell out of fashion and did not return until the conscious revivals of old styles in the nineteenth century.

By about 1700 English bond had been replaced – probably for aesthetic reasons – by what we call Flemish bond. Here, in each course of

8.8. Lytham Hall: Flemish Bond brickwork (of *c.*1760) with tuck pointing.

the outer face, a stretcher is followed by a header and so on, while, on the courses above and below, the laying is reversed, so that headers appear above and below stretchers, and vice versa – which produces a neat and attractive overall pattern [8.8]. Bricks in walls, which were never normally seen or which were on unimportant facades, were normally laid in what we call English garden wall bond, where a course of headers is topped by three (or five) courses of stretchers. Such work is quicker, and therefore cheaper, to build than English bond, let alone Flemish.

In most brickwork, where a very tidy appearance was not absolutely necessary, the mortar in which the bricks were laid was used to finish off the outer face – as is normal practice today. Until the advent of Portland cement in the 1850s this mortar appeared much whiter than the bricks, so that, if they were irregular or badly laid, the brickwork would look untidy. However, in good quality work the mortar which is seen on the outer face of a wall was only inserted carefully between the bricks – this is called 'pointing' – after the main mortar had begun to set. Various means were adopted to improve appearances (though brickwork never quite achieved the smooth finish of good ashlar stonework). The finer, but considerably more expensive way was to point the brickwork with a lime mortar to which brick-dust had been added, so that bricks and mortar had much the same colour, and then to score a pair of parallel lines in the still damp mortar, take out the mortar between them and replace it with a thin strip of lime putty to create a completely regular network of white lines. This 'tuck-pointing' can still be seen on the front of **Lytham Hall** [8.8]. The more usual (and much cheaper) way – which can be seen on the service wing at **Lytham** – was to score straight lines in a normal lime mortar, so that a network of slight and more or less regular shadows was created; its nickname, 'penny-struck pointing', hints at the method used.

Building technologies

Georgian

Georgian architects could be confident that their house designs would be carried out well, since they posed few structural problems and would, in most cases, be built by competent craftsmen, trained in a long tradition. Most architects rose from a craft background, serving first as a clerk of works and then 'leaving off their apron', as people said, and charging their client a fee of 5% of the cost of the works. While some of them were putting the clock back in terms of style, most of them were also willing, and sometimes eager, to introduce new technologies and materials into traditional masonry structures, whether of stone or brick.

First and foremost must be the sash windows, which replaced side-hung casements and which are perhaps the hallmark of Georgian houses in most people's eyes. They are complicated devices, involving very careful joiner's work to provide strong frames for the panes of glass, and also to ensure that the sashes, which are counter-weighted by lead cylinders hidden within the window frame, slide smoothly up and down and yet remain draught-proof.

The first of the new materials used in (later) Georgian houses was iron. It was always hidden [8.9], either in the form of cast-iron columns within a decorative casing of wood or false marble, or as wrought-iron beams (as above the wide stairhall at **Heaton**) or, sometimes, as wrought-iron straps to strengthen the treads and timber frame of a staircase. I have seen this at Barlaston Hall, near Stoke-on-Trent, but know of no Lancashire example.

Every significant Georgian house was built on a double-pile plan, and thought had to be taken about how to roof such deep buildings. The usual way at first was to place a normal pitched roof over the front half of the house, with the ends of its tie-beams resting on the front wall and on the middle wall between the front rooms and the back rooms, and then to build another parallel roof over the back half, and this can be seen at Leighton Hall. As taste increasingly demanded that roofs should be invisible from ground-level behind parapets or above projecting eaves, the problem was solved by placing a low and shallow-pitched roof — normally of slate from the Lake District or North Wales — over the outside rooms of a house, leaving a

8.9. Cast-iron posts once within timber columns.

lead-covered 'flat' roof over the central space, as is the case at Lytham Hall. This roof had to be drained, of course, and the necessary rainwater pipes, concealed within the house, have often caused problems – like the dry rot which attacked Rigmaden Park in the 1870s and 1920s, and led to the abandonment of the house after World War II.

Inside houses, timber-framed partition walls were often used, sometimes still with a wattle-and-daub infill early in the century, although laths, nailed to the timber frame and rendered with plaster, became common later. Laths were also used by c.1800 instead of straw as the base for plaster ceilings and, thanks to their relative lightness, were also used for creating decorative features like cornices and niches [8.10].

After about 1770 external decorative work with repeated motifs was increasingly carried out in the newly invented Coade stone. This was a form of frost-resistant, normally stone-coloured terra cotta and was produced, like bricks, in moulds at a factory in London. Its manufacturer, Eleanor Coade, insisted on high standards and commissioned well-known artists to produce fine designs for the moulds. Coade stone was expensive, but cheaper than hand-carved work. We now know that it was also very durable – as the bas-reliefs on the garden façade at **Heaton Hall** show well, despite aggressive stone-cleaning in the 1980s.

Towards the end of the eighteenth century came the invention of a number of 'cements', which were used to render brick houses in the hope of making walls more rain-resistant and of giving them the appearance of ashlar stonework – especially if the render were incised with horizontal and vertical lines to mimic the joints between blocks of stone. Most cements did not adhere very well to the underlying bricks, and it is doubtful that any renders have survived for two centuries. Nevertheless, **Astley Hall** and **Dallam Tower** provide good examples of render applied to older brickwork, while the 1840 wing at **Holker** was rendered and lined out from the start.

8.10. Plaster on laths to create decorative details (of c.1830).

Victorian

With very few exceptions Lancashire gentry houses, designed during the nineteenth century, were built of brick and then faced with ashlar stonework, fixed to the bricks with the aid of wrought-iron cramps. This can be well seen in the ruins of **Grove House**, Allerton [8.11]. This method made for faster construction and allowed the use of impressively-sized facing stones, but such stones were very often wrongly bedded – that is, their 'bedding plane' (which corresponds to the way in which the stone was laid down originally as a sediment and should therefore be horizontal) is instead vertical – with the result that they tend to weather badly. What is more, if water penetrates such masonry, the iron cramps eventually rust and expand and force parts of the face of the stone to flake off. Thurnham Hall had to be totally refaced in the 1970s for this reason.

The early nineteenth century saw the introduction of new materials and techniques, like bronze frames for large sash windows, or cast-iron for glazing conservatories and other utilitarian buildings. Hidden wrought-iron beams had long been used to strengthen, or to replace, softwood timber beams, but sometimes this structural ironwork is also visible and decorative. A good and attractive example is at **Leighton Hall**, where the cast-iron screen in the hall at the foot of the stairs also carries the floor joists of the upper corridor. [6.12]

8.11. Grove House, Allerton: ashlar facing to a brick wall.

Glass was first cast into sheets in England in 1773 at Ravenhead, near St Helens, but techniques improved only slowly. However, by the 1840s it was possible to replace the timber glazing bars and fairly small panes, which are typical of Georgian sash windows, with large sheets of plate glass; this development was encouraged by the removal of taxes on glass in 1845 and on windows in 1851. For a generation or so most people believed that large windows and large panes improved the appearance of a house, as well as the view from it, but smaller panes and even leaded panes came back into fashion in the 1880s and 1890s, as taste became more self-consciously backward-looking. **Holker** and **Blackwell** show good examples of this new fashion.

8.12. Leighton Hall:
bells (*c*.1820) and
electric bells (*c*.1930)

'Modern conveniences' within Georgian and Victorian houses

Life in gentry houses became more comfortable for more people during
the eighteenth and nineteenth centuries.

A luxury of living in Georgian and Victorian times was provided by
the use of ice, which could be collected in winter from a lake in the park
and then stored – packed between layers of straw – in an ice house, sunk
half-underground in a well-shaded spot. This was normally a brick-lined
circular pit with a domed roof – rather like a large egg about six metres
tall – with a drain at the bottom and an entrance on one side towards
the top. Many gentry houses had an ice house, but they are now quite
hard to find. There is one hidden away behind Scarisbrick Hall, and
another about 100 metres north west of Towneley Hall, almost invisible
in a north-facing slope. However, the icehouse at Lytham, which is
known to have existed near to a large pond in the grounds, has not yet
been found.

A convenient feature inside later Georgian houses was provided by
bell-wires, which meant that it was no longer necessary for a servant or
two to stand all the time in the hall of the house. Instead, by turning a
handle in a family room, a bell of a certain pitch was rung in or near the
servants' hall, to summon a servant to that room. The arrangement was
probably liked among servants, and, as far as the family was concerned,
it allowed the entire house to be dedicated to their private use. Perhaps
the best surviving example in Lancashire of such bells is at **Leighton
Hall** [8.12].

Throughout the Georgian period candles were the most common form of lighting. Beeswax candles have a sweet smell. Tallow candles were much cheaper but, because they were made of animal fat, smelt rather like burnt hamburgers. In Victorian times they were often superseded by oil lamps, and later both were gradually replaced by gas lighting; this was, however, unpleasantly hot and smelly until the introduction of incandescent mantles in the 1880s. Gas was normally produced from coal in a small gas-works on the estate; the buildings of one survive, with the base of the gas-holder, about 100 metres behind Scarisbrick Hall.

Water closets of sorts had been available since Elizabethan times, but U-bends with a water-trap to cut out sewer-smells were not introduced until the middle of the nineteenth century. Only then did close stools become a thing of the past. Hot-water central heating was also introduced about then – the ornate brass grilles at floor level, which hide the hot-water pipes, can be seen in several rooms at **Scarisbrick**.

By the end of the century a number of houses had bathrooms, and a few had (low-voltage) electric lights, as at **Blackwell,** and at **Holker** where in the library the switches are hidden behind false book spines. By 1900 some gentry houses had become nearly as comfortable as the houses we now live in.

References

[1]   Thomas Fuller, *The Holy State* (1642) p. 167.
[2]   John Champness, 'The Building of Gawthorpe Hall' in *Contrebis* (vol 31, 2006–7), pp. 33–41.
[3]   Peter de Figueiredo and Julian Treuherz, *Cheshire Country Houses* (1988), p. 92.

Further Reading

Chapter One: medieval origins

There is further (mainly architectural) information on all the houses mentioned in this book in the revised Lancashire volumes in Pevsner's *Buildings of England* series – namely *Manchester and the South East* by Clare Hartwell and Matthew Hyde (2004), *Liverpool and the South West* by Richard Pollard (2006) and *North Lancashire* by Clare Hartwell (2009). *Cumbria* by Matthew Hyde was published in November 2010, and the volume on *Cheshire,* by Clare Hartwell and Matthew Hyde, should appear in 2011.

In addition to articles in the relevant volumes of Pevsner's *Buildings of England,* the best and most accessible introduction to medieval houses, built for the gentry (and others) is Anthony Emery, *Discovering Medieval Houses* (2007). Emery has also written *Greater Medieval Houses in England and Wales,* and in volume 1 (1996) gives more detailed information on Ashton Hall, Beetham Hall, Chetham's Hospital, Middleton Hall, Ordsall Hall, Rufford Old Hall, Smithills Hall, Towneley Hall, Turton Tower and Warton Old Rectory.

There are house guides at Rufford Old Hall, Towneley Hall and Turton Tower, while the architecture and history of Chetham's Hospital are described in Clare Hartwell's *Manchester* in the Pevsner Architectural Guides (2001) and, much more fully, in her book, *The History and Architecture of Chetham's School and Library* (2004).

Chapter Two: the sixteenth century

In addition to articles in the relevant volumes of Pevsner's *Buildings of England,* there are house guides at Astley Hall, Browsholme Hall, Gawthorpe Hall, Hoghton Tower, Levens Hall, Little Moreton Hall, Sizergh Castle, Speke Hall, Towneley Hall and Turton Tower.

Nicholas Cooper, *Houses of the Gentry 1480–1680* (1999), is the best introduction to the gentry houses of those two centuries.

Mark Girouard, *Elizabethan Architecture – Its Rise and Fall, 1540–1640* (2009) is now the standard work, but his earlier *Robert Smythson and the Elizabethan Country House* (1983) is still worth reading.

Malcolm Airs, *The Tudor and Jacobean Country House* (1995) is interesting. As its subtitle, *A Building History*, implies, it is largely concerned with the building process. Although the houses mentioned are mainly in the South and Midlands, the picture is nation-wide.

Chapter Three: the seventeenth century

In addition to articles in the relevant volumes of Pevsner's *Buildings of England*, there are house guides at Astley Hall, Gawthorpe Hall, Hall i' th' Wood, Hoghton Tower, the Judges' Lodgings in Lancaster, Levens Hall, Rufford Old Hall and Towneley Hall.

W. John and Kit Smith, *An Architectural History of Towneley Hall, Burnley* (2004) and Nicholas Cooper, *Houses of the Gentry 1480–1680*, (1999) are also valuable.

Nicholas Cooper has also written *The Jacobean House* (2007), which is lavishly illustrated with photographs published in *Country Life*.

Chapter Four: estates in the long eighteenth century

There are three books worth reading on country houses and their estates: firstly, Heather A. Clemenson, who set the ball rolling with her *English Country Houses and Landed Estates* (1982) and then two illustrated books: John Martin Robinson's *The English Country Estate* (1988), and *Property and Landscape* (1987) by Tom Williamson and Liz Bellamy, which covers a wider field.

Chapter Five: the eighteenth century

In addition to articles in the relevant volumes of Pevsner's *Buildings of England*, there are house guides at Dunham Massey, Heaton Hall, the Judges' Lodgings in Lancaster, Lytham Hall, Platt Hall, Tabley Hall, Tatton Park and Towneley Hall – for which there is also John and Kit Smith's interesting book, *An Architectural History of Towneley Hall* (2004)

Probably the best introduction to eighteenth-century houses is still to be found in the relevant chapters of John Summerson's *Architecture in Britain, 1530–1830* (1991). A fuller treatment is Giles Worsley's *Classical Architecture in Britain – The Heroic Age* (1995). Also of considerable interest are *Creating Paradise – the Building of the English Country House, 1660–1880* by Richard Wilson and Alan Mackley (2000), and Christopher Christie's *The British Country House in the Eighteenth Century* (2000). All, however, concentrate on aristocratic houses rather than on gentry houses.

Chapter Six: the nineteenth century

In addition to articles in the relevant volumes of Pevsner's *Buildings of England,* there are house guides at Blackwell, Browsholme Hall, Conishead Priory, Gawthorpe Hall, Hoghton Tower, Leighton Hall, Levens Hall, Rufford Old Hall, Scarisbrick Hall, Towneley Hall and Turton Tower.

The standard work on the (mostly larger) houses of the period is still Mark Girouard, *The Victorian Country House* (1979), but it can now be supplemented by Michael Hall, *The Victorian Country House* (2009) which is beautifully illustrated from *Country Life* and contains an article on Scarisbrick Hall.

Equally interesting on later (and mostly smaller) houses is *Arts and Crafts Architecture* (1997) by Peter Davey.

The varied plans of Victorian houses have been carefully analysed and described in Jill Franklin, *The Gentleman's Country House and its Plan* (1981)

The life of the family and staff in a large gentry house is well portrayed in *The Edwardian Country House* by Juliet Gardiner (2002).

Chapter Seven: the twentieth century

In addition to articles in the relevant volumes of Pevsner's *Buildings of England,* there is a house guide at Meols Hall, and further information on the house in three books, Clive Aslet, *The Last Country Houses (1982),* John Martin Robinson*, The Latest Country Houses* (1984) and John Cornforth, *The Inspiration of the Past* (1985)

Three interesting books on the recent history of country houses generally are: John Cornforth, *The Country Houses of England 1948–98* (1998); David Littlejohn, *The Fate of the English Country House* (1997); and Peter Mandler, *The Fall and Rise of the Stately Home* (1997).

Appendix

Alec Clifton-Taylor, *The Pattern of English Building* (1987) is widely regarded as the best of all books on the building materials used in traditional domestic architecture.

More detailed descriptions of the main building materials and their uses are Richard Harris, *Discovering Timber-framed Buildings* (2004); Alec Clifton-Taylor and A.S. Ireson, *English Stone Building* (1994); and R. W. Brunskill, *Brick Building in Britain* (1990)

On the building process itself Malcolm Airs' interesting book, *The Tudor and Jacobean Country House – A Building History*, goes well beyond his narrow dates.

General

There are short articles, including a few plans, on most of the older houses mentioned in this book in the various volumes of the *Victoria County History of Lancashire,* which was published between 1906 and 1914. Some of the information is out-of-date and inaccurate, but for anyone who hopes to make a serious study of Lancashire country houses, the *VCH* is a useful starting point – though no more.

The magazine *Country Life* is an essential starting point, since several issues contain articles on houses mentioned in this book. Some of the information in pre-war issues is out-of-date and inaccurate, but all are well illustrated and worth reading. Up to the end of March 2011, the relevant articles, and publication dates, are:

Astley Hall (8, 15 and 22 June 1922);
Borwick Hall (20 May 1911, and 10 August 1935);
Browsholme Hall (13 July 1935);
Burrow Hall (14 and 21 April 1960);
Gawthorpe Hall (10 May 1913, and 4 and 11 September 1975);
Heaton Hall (10 December 1992);
Hoghton Tower (23 and 30 July 1992);
Holker Hall (26 June and 2 July 1980);
Houses of the Lune Valley (28 January and 4 February 1982);
Hutton-in-the-Forest (15 March 2007);
Ince Blundell Hall (10, 17 and 24 April 1958);
Leighton Hall (11 and 18 May 1951);
Levens Hall (6 December 2001);
Little Moreton Hall (1 April 2009);
Lytham Hall (21 and 28 July 1960);
Meols Hall (25 January and 1 February 1973);
Rigmaden Park (10 June 2004);
Rufford Old Hall (19 and 26 October 1929);
Scarisbrick Hall (13 and 20 March 1958, and 8 and 15 August 2002);
Sizergh Castle (22 June 2000);
Smithills Hall (2 March 1995);
Speke Hall (23 April 1987);
Stonyhurst College (15 and 22 October 1910); and
Towneley Hall (19 February 1998).

Further articles may be available, in due course, at www.country life.co.uk

Two books on Lancashire houses, which are worth reading, are David Brazendale's *Lancashire's Historic Halls* (2005), which complements this book by looking briefly at a couple of dozen older gentry houses, and using them as pegs on which to hang essays on topics from the county's social and economic history; and then John Martin Robinson's encyclopaedic gazetteer, *A Guide to the Country Houses of the North West* (1991).

Anyone wanting to undertake any serious study of the owners and estates related to country houses should read *Researching the Country House* by Arthur Elton, Brett Harrison and Keith Wark (1992).

On the architecture of country houses generally my 'Bible' is Geoffrey Tyack's and Steven Brindle's *Blue Guide: Country Houses of England* (1994), which gives scholarly descriptions of about four hundred houses. Simon Jenkins' *England's Thousand Best Houses* (2003) is also well worth dipping into; some of his comments are controversial, but all are worth considering.

Perhaps the best book on gardens is Christopher Thacker, *England's Historic Gardens* (1989); it deals with the 'hundred best', so the only 'Lancashire' garden mentioned is at Levens.

Finally, if I had to choose only one book to recommend, it would be Mark Girouard's beautifully written *Life in the English Country House* (1978, but still in print). It will inspire you to read many more.

Indices

Index of Houses

Numbers in the left-hand margin correspond to the numbers on the map
(on p. xiv) which show the approximate location of houses.

Houses in 'Lancashire' which are visible from a public highway are –
whether open to the public or not – given a grid reference, e.g. 103/76.27.

Houses in 'Lancashire' which are normally open to visitors are **printed
in bold**.

Houses in 'Lancashire' which are visible but private are marked (P).

Page numbers given at the end of the entry in *italics* indicate illustrations.

Index of People

Including builders (name of house is given in brackets), architects and craftsmen.

General Index